HAUNTED KIDS

Bruce Nash and Allan Zullo
with Ray Villwock

Watermill Press

To Peter Skolnik, who started it all and is still with me in spirit.
— Bruce Nash

To Tommy Ryder, the nicest ghost I ever knew.
— Allan Zullo

Library of Congress Cataloging-in-Publication Data

Nash, Bruce M.
    Haunted kids / Bruce Nash and Allan Zullo, with Ray Villwock.
        p.   cm.
    Summary: Eleven tales, based in part on reported cases, of
children's encounters with the supernatural.
    ISBN 0-8167-3444-3 (pbk.)
    1. Ghost stories—Juvenile literature. [1. Ghosts.] I. Zullo,
Allan.   II. Villwock, Ray.   III. Title.
BF1461.N37   1994
133.1—dc20
                                                                        93-14489

Published by Watermill Press, an imprint of Troll Associates, Inc.
Copyright © 1994 by Nash and Zullo Productions, Inc.
Printed in the United States of America.
10   9   8   7   6   5   4   3   2   1

CONTENTS

INTRODUCTION

Do ghosts really exist?

No one can prove they do. But on the other hand, no one can prove they don't!

There are many people — including kids — who claim they not only saw ghosts but actually were haunted by them.

In many cases, experts were called in to investigate these so-called hauntings. Usually, the experts walked away baffled. All they knew for sure was something strange had happened that could not fully be explained.

This book contains 11 chilling stories based, in part, on real cases taken from the files of experienced ghost hunters. The names and places in the stories have been changed to protect everyone's privacy.

When it comes to ghosts, there's a thin line between a scary tale and a startling truth. Are you brave enough to cross it?

THE DEVIL'S GARDEN

Lilly Mayfield first sensed the presence of the strange girl shortly after her family moved into the weathered old house.

Lilly's dad, a bulldozer operator, and her mom, a waitress, always wanted to live in the country. They finally had scraped up enough money to buy the house. It was in need of repair because it had remained empty for several years, but Lilly didn't mind. After living in a cramped apartment in town all her life, the nine-year-old finally had a room of her own and didn't have to share it with her 11-year-old brother Curtis.

The house, built in a stand of scrub pines in north Florida, sported a front porch where Lilly loved to sway on the swinging bench. From her vantage point, she could watch deer, raccoons, foxes, possums, and all kinds of birds. And the prettiest, most colorful butterflies she had ever seen.

Lilly was on that porch when she first heard the giggling of a girl. It sounded as though it came from the yard, even though no one was there. Some days Lilly heard laughter; other days snickers and sometimes humming. But it was always the same voice. At first, she thought Curtis was playing a joke on her. But Lilly often heard the giggles when Curtis was off fishing or had gone into town with his dad.

1

She asked her parents if they had heard the girl, but they simply shook their heads and shrugged it off as the voice of an imaginary friend.

But Lilly knew better — especially after the weird incidents in the kitchen.

One day, only a few weeks after they had moved in, Curtis stomped out onto the porch and snapped, "Lilly, did you take my sandwich?"

"No, why?"

"Don't lie," he said. "I fixed a peanut butter and jelly sandwich, and then I went to get some milk. When I had my back turned, you swiped it."

"I did not," she protested. "I've been here the whole time. You're crazy."

The next day, while her parents were working out in the yard, Lilly poured herself a full glass of milk and then went into the pantry to grab a couple of cookies. When she returned, the glass was half empty.

"Curtis!" she cried. "You know how I hate it when you drink from my glass! Curtis, where are you?"

"I'm upstairs," he shouted back. "So unless I'm Superman and flew into the kitchen and back without you seeing me, I didn't touch your drink."

Just then Lilly thought she heard a faint, high-pitched "tee-hee-tee-hee."

If it had happened only once, Lilly probably would have ignored it. But other goodies and drinks had mysteriously disappeared from both kids' plates and glasses. It was usually only a cracker, a cookie, maybe some raisins, or gulps of soda. And always there was that haunting giggle — a strange little laugh even Curtis began to hear, although at first he refused to admit it to his younger sister.

Sometimes when Lilly was upstairs alone in her room,

she'd get the uneasy feeling that someone was watching her. And an eerie breeze would suddenly chill the warm, humid air in her room for just a moment.

About a month after the Mayfields moved in, Lilly saw the little girl for the first time.

Early one Sunday morning, before her parents or brother had awakened, Lilly shuffled into the kitchen and popped a piece of bread into the toaster. As she waited for the toast, she had the feeling she wasn't alone. She turned around and sucked in a startled breath. Staring at her from the other side of the screen door was a twinkle-eyed, pudgy-cheeked girl who looked about the same age as Lilly. Her dark skin contrasted sharply to the white sleeveless blouse and shorts she wore. Her black, wiry hair was twisted into two long pigtails tied with big white bows.

Before Lilly could utter a sound, the girl winked and broke into a wide toothy grin. Then she faded away. A moment later, Lilly heard her giggle.

Lilly wasn't scared. She was just stunned at what she saw — or what she *thought* she saw. Only when a whiff of smoke tickled her nose did she jump.

The toast! She had forgotten about the toast, which was now burning to a crisp in the old, broken-down toaster. After unplugging the appliance and fishing out the burnt bread, Lilly heard that faint "tee-hee-tee-hee" again.

She raced upstairs and shook her slumbering brother. "Curtis! Curtis! Wake up! I saw her! I saw her!"

"What are you talking about?" he mumbled.

"The girl! You know, the one who giggles and steals our food. I think she's a ghost!"

Curtis sat up in bed and rubbed his eyes. "Lilly, are you sure you weren't dreaming?"

"I swear to you, I saw her in the kitchen just now. She

3

was standing in the doorway and then she just disappeared — right in front of me! You believe me, don't you?"

"Well, maybe ... I don't know. Now listen. Don't go telling Mom or Dad. They already think you're half crazy with your make-believe friend."

"She's not make-believe. She's real — a real ghost!"

"Whatever you say." He yawned and stretched. "I might as well get up now and get ready. After breakfast, Dad is taking me to the Devil's Garden."

The Devil's Garden was a large cypress swamp about a 30-minute walk from the house. The kids were under strict orders not to go near the swamp without an adult. They were told it was a dangerous place, full of snakes, alligators, and deep pockets of muck and water that could swallow people whole.

Curtis couldn't stand having such a fascinating place so nearby and not being able to see it. So he kept pestering his father to take him until finally his dad agreed. Unfortunately for Lilly, her dad felt she was too young to go there. But he promised to take her when she was a little older.

When father and son returned later that afternoon from the Devil's Garden, Curtis excitedly described the swamp to Lilly. "We saw gators so big they could gobble you up in one bite! And cypress trees with these weird roots sticking out of the water. And mean old water snakes by the dozen. And the strangest-looking plants you've ever seen. It was like from way back in time. I half expected to see a dinosaur or something. It was so cool!"

"I want to go next time," said Lilly.

"No way! It's too dangerous. It's no place for a girl."

That dumb remark only made Lilly more determined than ever to see the Devil's Garden. For the next couple of

4

weeks, she repeatedly begged Curtis to take her there even though she knew their parents had forbidden them to go near the swamp alone.

"You know, it's no big deal you saw the swamp, because Dad took you there," Lilly taunted her brother. "If you're so big and brave, you ought to go to the swamp with me. I'll be good. I won't run off or anything."

"Okay, okay," he said. "But you've got to promise not to tell Mom or Dad, or we'll be in for some heavy-duty punishment."

———

Curtis led his sister along a path through the scrub pine until they reached what looked like an enormous curtain of leafy vines draped over the trees. "Wait 'til you see what's on the other side," Curtis told her. He parted the vines as Lilly eagerly stepped through.

The moment her eyes gazed upon the wondrous emerald kingdom, Lilly fell in love with the place. Streams of light filtering through the tall trees lit up the green leafy ferns, red air plants, and bright white and yellow orchids. Long trains of blue-gray Spanish moss dangled from the branches like lace.

Fat, red-bellied turtles sunned themselves on logs while elegant white herons waded in the water, searching for tadpoles and other small fish. The swamp pulsed with the sounds of croaking frogs, squawking birds, and buzzing insects.

Lilly began to enter the swamp, gingerly stepping in muck and moss-covered ground, and squealing with delight at each new marvel.

"Lilly, get back here," Curtis ordered. "You're going in too far."

"Oh, don't be such a baby," she said. Her eyes then locked on a huge swallowtail butterfly adorned with a bright yellow band and blue dots. She had never seen such a butterfly and began chasing it as it flitted from flower to flower.

Suddenly Lilly let out a bloodcurdling scream. Curtis raced over and saw what had frightened her. Only a few feet away, a nasty five-foot (1.5-m)-long snake reared its ugly head, opened its mouth wide, and bared its deadly fangs.

"It's a cottonmouth!" yelled Curtis. "If it bites you, you could die!" The two ran for their lives, frantically weaving their way through the cypress, plowing into sticky spider webs, and splashing in ankle-deep mud. They finally staggered to a halt and plopped onto a log, trying to catch their breath.

"Let's get out of here, okay?" said Lilly.

"Fine with me," said Curtis. He looked to his left and right. Then he turned around.

"Curtis, which way do we go?"

"Uh, I think this way." He really didn't have a clue to the way out of the swamp. But he didn't want to scare Lilly any more than she already was.

After an hour of hiking through the swamp, Lilly began to whimper. "We're lost, aren't we?" she asked.

"I'm not sure," he mumbled. "Well, maybe."

"I'm scared," said Lilly as tears rolled down her face. "I want to go home."

The swamp didn't seem so beautiful anymore. The light was beginning to fade. The greens were turning into shades of brown. The noises seemed louder and more menacing. The pretty butterflies and dragonflies had been replaced by attacking mosquitoes and horseflies.

"We've got to keep walking," said Curtis, grabbing his

sister's hand. "This way." They stepped on what they thought was solid ground. But it was water lettuce — a vegetation that spreads out like a thick green carpet and floats over the water. It looks solid, but it isn't.

Curtis and Lilly tumbled into knee-deep murky water. A few yards away, they heard an enormous splash. Then they saw something large and gray swim toward them. It had a broad, rounded snout, big eyes, and ridges on its back.

"It's a gator!" Curtis shouted.

They clawed their way through the water lettuce, scrambled to solid ground, and once again fled in panic. Then Lilly saw something that made her stop in her tracks.

"Look, Curtis, up ahead! It's a person!" Leaning against a holly tree, clad in a sleeveless white blouse and shorts, was the pudgy-faced girl. "It's the ghost!" exclaimed Lilly. "It's the girl I was telling you about!"

"Don't be silly," Curtis said. Facing the girl, he asked, "Who are you?"

She didn't answer. Instead, she broke into a sweet smile and beckoned them to follow her. They didn't budge. She took a few steps, turned, and motioned with her hand again.

"Let's follow her, Curtis," said Lilly. "I have a feeling she knows the way out of here."

For the next half hour, the silent girl led them on a twisting course through the Devil's Garden, stopping every so often to point out where they should and shouldn't step. Finally, to Lilly and Curtis's everlasting joy, they emerged from the swamp.

"Thank you, thank you so much," Lilly told the girl. "You saved our lives."

The girl gave a silly grin, a big wink ... and then slowly vanished before their eyes. And then she giggled.

7

Lilly and Curtis never saw her again.

———————

About six years later, Lilly was doing the spring cleaning for Mrs. Dillard, an elderly widow who lived a couple of miles down the road. The two were taking a break for lunch when Mrs. Dillard began talking about the good old days.

"I remember when the house you're living in was built," she told Lilly. "Logan was his name, Henry Lee Logan. He was a wizard with his hands. Spent over two years putting that house together for his family.

"Why, I believe I have a picture of your house back then. Go in the closet and fetch me that red album — the one that's marked '1950s'." Lilly did what she was told and pulled her chair next to Mrs. Dillard at the dining room table. "Let's see," said the woman, flipping through the pages. "Oh yes, here it is, with the whole Logan family standing on the front porch."

Lilly looked at the photo with some interest and smiled. The house looked so spiffy and new, not like it was now with the paint peeling and the porch posts leaning. And the family in the photo looked so proud. Mrs. Dillard was about to close the album when Lilly caught sight of something that stirred an intense feeling inside her.

"Wait," she said, gently grabbing Mrs. Dillard's hand. Lilly closely examined the photo of the Logan family — Henry, his wife, two boys ... and a girl about nine years old. She had pigtails tied up in ribbons, a wide toothy grin, and pudgy cheeks.

"I know this girl!" Lilly said excitedly. "I've seen her before."

"Land sakes, child, that's impossible," said Mrs. Dillard. "That's Louisa Ann Logan, the sweetest, most lov-

8

able little lady you'd ever want to meet. Always laughing and giggling. But she died before you were even born."

"How?"

"Oh, it was a real tragedy is what it was. She always wanted to visit the Devil's Garden, but her daddy told her not until she got older would he take her. Well, that spunky little thing went off on her own one day to the swamp. She never came back. They searched for days in that swamp, but all they found was one of her white ribbons and a shoe. Folks around here say she stepped in some water lettuce, fell in the water, and got eaten by a gator." Lilly was so stunned she didn't even hear Mrs. Dillard continue.

"The Logans were real broken up. After a while, they couldn't stand to live there anymore and they moved on. The strangest thing, though. Every now and then someone comes back from the Devil's Garden and swears they've heard a little girl giggling just like Louisa Ann."

GRAVE CONSEQUENCES

Tim Murphy knew there was something evil about that cemetery the very first day he stood in front of it. Peering from beyond the rusty iron gates that guarded its entrance, Tim saw a cemetery unlike any he had ever known before.

Instead of neatly arranged tombstones lining a mowed green lawn, this graveyard was a jumble of chipped, weather-stained monuments leaning this way and that among patches of yellowed grass, dirt, and weeds.

The 11-year-old boy and his mother Jayne had just moved into an apartment right across the street from the forbidding cemetery. Their new home was a cramped two-bedroom apartment in an old section of an industrial town near Boston. It was all his mother could afford following her divorce. At least it was convenient. Tim could catch the school bus two blocks away, and she could walk the six blocks to the factory where she worked.

During the first few days in his new surroundings, Tim strolled through the graveyard even though his mother had told him to stay away. Although the place gave him goose bumps, he found it kind of thrilling to feel a little spooked. Other than a few homeless people, he never saw anyone visit the place or tend to the grounds.

Judging from the most recent dates on the tombstones, Tim figured there hadn't been a burial there in 20 years. As he wandered around, he read the inscriptions on the gravestones and wondered who the people were, what they looked like, and how they died.

"George Bigelow, Beloved Husband and Father, Born February 12, 1842, Died May 7, 1910." . . . "Sweet Infant Sarah Kelly Fitzpatrick, Who Brought Joy on this Earth, April 15, 1825-October 10, 1825." . . . "In Loving Memory, Mary Margaret Evans, 1823-1905." . . . "Timothy Murphy, 1903-1917."

Tim froze in his tracks and gulped. *That's my name!*

He looked closer to make sure he wasn't imagining things. The stone marker was typical for that cemetery, only smaller, about two feet tall and rounded at the top. Decades of soot had blackened the edges, and the harsh weather had eroded some of the lettering. Two jagged cracks shaped like lightning bolts sliced through the "T" in "Timothy" and the "p" in "Murphy." But there was no mistaking the name. It was Tim's.

The thought of seeing his own name carved on a tombstone sent a shiver up his spine. There was nothing else written on the marker to give Tim any clue about the person who shared his name. *He must have come from a poor family to have such a small gravestone,* Tim thought. *He was only 14 years old. That's just three years older than me. I wonder how he died. Was he sick? Did he drown? Maybe he was murdered!*

The more Tim looked at the marker, the more uneasy he felt. It gave him the willies. In fact, he didn't ever want to see the tombstone again. It was just too weird to have a marker standing there with his name on it. So with a grunt, Tim pushed hard against the stone. It took him a couple of tries, but finally he managed to topple it over face down.

Then he started to run off, looking over his shoulder to see if anybody had witnessed what he had done. By the time he returned home, he figured he'd never have to think about that gravestone and the late Timothy Murphy again.

But he was wrong — dead wrong.

That night, while sleeping in his room, Tim was awakened by an eerie sound, a kind of moaning that repeatedly grew louder and then softer. He jerked up in bed and turned his head from side to side, trying to find the source. But the moaning seemed to be everywhere . . . yet nowhere.

Before Tim had time to get any more scared than he already was, his bed began to rock and sway silently as if it was bobbing on the ocean. Clutching the side of his bed, Tim tried to scream for help, but nothing came out of his mouth. He tried again, this time at the top of his lungs. "Mom! Mom! Make it stop! Make it stop!"

Jayne Murphy rushed into his room and flipped on the light. "What's wrong, Timmy?"

"Didn't you hear that strange sound?" the terrified boy asked. "Didn't you see my bed move?"

"What are you talking about, honey?"

He told her about the awful moaning and how his bed had rocked by itself. She had seen and heard nothing. However, Jayne clearly noticed the terror in her son's eyes.

"Sweetheart, it was just a nightmare, that's all," she said. "You probably got some creepy thoughts from playing in the cemetery. Promise me you'll stay away from there. Now," she added as she straightened out his blanket, "try to go back to sleep and think pleasant thoughts. I'll leave your door open and the bathroom light on. Good night, sweetie. I love you."

Tim felt foolish that he had cried out for his mother. *Maybe she was right. Maybe it was all a bad dream.* He didn't sleep well the rest of the night. When he got up the next morning, he thought his conscience had played a trick on him because he had overturned the gravestone.

Just to be on the safe side, maybe if I go to the cemetery and put the marker back, I won't have that bad dream again.

Tim trudged through the old cemetery gates, trying to convince himself that the horror from the previous night was a figment of his imagination. But he still had a queasy feeling in his stomach. *Somehow this isn't over yet,* he told himself.

As he neared the fallen gravestone, Tim stopped dead in his tracks. A boy was standing right next to Timothy Murphy's marker — and he hadn't been there a second ago. It was as if he had appeared out of thin air. And there was something else odd about him — his clothes were from another time.

The boy looked about 14 years old, stocky, with red curly hair sticking out from under a tweed cap — the kind you'd see in an old movie. He wore black work boots, wool pants with the cuffs rolled up, and a dirty white shirt that was torn and tattered . . . and bloody. But even worse, his right arm was missing and his shoulder was soaked in blood! The boy squinted his eyes, grimaced in pain, and let out a spine-tingling moan — the same sound Tim had heard the night before!

Seized with fear, Tim spun on his heels and ran through the monuments, past the cemetery gates, across the street, into the apartment building, and up the two flights of stairs to his floor before he dared turn around. He fumbled in his pocket for the key and had trouble unlocking the door to his apartment because his hands were trembling so much. Finally, he whipped inside and slammed and bolted the door.

With his heart pounding, Tim waited for someone — or something — to come. Several minutes went by before he timidly walked to the window and peeked outside at the cemetery. No one was there. He then checked each room of the house. Nothing. Tim breathed a sigh of relief, thankful that his mother was at work so he didn't have to explain what had happened.

But what did happen? Was it a prank? Was it my imagination? Or did I just see a ghost? Could that have been the ghost of the Timothy Murphy who died? Tim didn't have the answers. But he knew one thing. He was never, *ever* going back to that cemetery!

That night, Tim didn't want to go to bed because he was still afraid. He wanted to stay up as late as he could. Because it wasn't a school night and his mother was tired from working all day, she let Tim watch television while she went to sleep. About 1:00 A.M., Tim stumbled into bed, making sure his door was open and the bathroom light was on. Then he drifted off to sleep.

Just before dawn, Tim was jarred awake by that same dreadful moaning. He threw the covers over his head, but the moaning only intensified. And then Tim's flesh started to crawl when he felt the bed move again, slowly at first and then rocking back and forth until it burst into a violent shaking fit. As Tim held on to his bed for dear life, the covers flew off. What he saw horrified him. There, hovering at the end of his bed, was the moaning one-armed boy! He was staring at Tim with such fury that Tim was sure he was going to kill him!

Before Tim could utter a sound, the lurching bed pitched him onto the floor. Just then his mother burst

14

into the room.

"Timmy!" she screamed. "What's happening?"

"It's a ghost!" Tim cried. "Look out!"

She quickly scanned the room but saw nothing at first. The ghost had vanished. The bed had stopped shaking. But now she too could hear the awful moaning.

Next came the shock of their lives. The chair to Tim's desk zipped across the room — by itself — and crashed into the door. The bed began to vibrate again and bang repeatedly into the wall. A huge poster of a basketball star taped to the wall was suddenly torn in two by invisible hands. Tim's school books flew through the air like crazed birds, knocking over his bedside lamp. And one by one the clothes in his closet were ripped from their hangers. Next, Tim's radio shattered as if an unseen iron fist had pounded on it. And through it all Tim and Jayne Murphy heard the moaning rising and falling in eerie waves.

Then, as unexpectedly as it began, the terrifying ordeal ended. Tim and his mother found themselves on their knees, clutching each other. They were too frightened and shocked to utter a sound for several minutes.

"This can't be happening," Jayne finally said. "I can't believe what I just saw." The stunned mother and son staggered out into the living room and collapsed onto the couch. They tried to make sense of what they had just experienced, but they couldn't.

"Maybe we should call the police," said Jayne.

"Mom, no one's going to believe us. They'll think we're nuts."

Just then, the moaning started again. And from inside the walls, a loud pounding sound assaulted their ears.

"Mom, I'm so scared. Let's get out of here — now!"

Jayne grabbed her petrified son by the hand and ran

15

across the hall. She banged on the door of their neighbors, Jack and Lynn Grayson. The sleepy-eyed couple opened the door and were shocked by the terror-stricken faces of the Murphys.

"What's all the commotion?" Jack asked. "Who's doing all that banging?"

When Jayne told them of the violent force that had invaded their home, Jack, a hulking steelworker, marched into their apartment. Two minutes later, he returned with his eyes wide and his voice trembling. "Something bad is in there, real bad. The walls and floor were vibrating like an earthquake. And a chair in the kitchen flipped right on its back before my very eyes. Your place is haunted!"

"Stay with us for now," Lynn told the Murphys. "I have a friend who knows a psychic investigator. I'll call in the morning. Let's see if he can figure out what to do."

But Tim already knew what to do. He knew what had caused the moaning, the shaking bed, the destruction of his room, the banging walls. It was the ghost of Timothy Murphy.

It took all morning for Tim to muster up the courage to go back to the cemetery. When he reached the graveyard gates, his feet felt like lead, and his stomach was twisted in knots. But he made himself march past the rows of stark monuments. He was hoping the one-armed ghost wasn't hiding behind one of them.

When he was about a half a football field away from Timothy Murphy's tombstone, he stopped. He had never felt such fear in his life. He was desperately fighting the urge to turn around and run home. But he knew he couldn't.

I've got to do this or that ghost will haunt us forever — or kill us, Tim told himself. He took a deep breath and then dashed straight for the gravestone. His eyes darted back

16

and forth as he ran to the marker, because he didn't want to be surprised if the one-armed boy suddenly appeared.

Without wasting a second, Tim lifted up the tombstone and put it back just as he found it, securing it with some rocks and dirt. Then he stepped back and said out loud, "Look, I'm really sorry I tipped over your gravestone. I didn't mean to cause any trouble. It's just that you and I have the same name, and I didn't want to have my name on a tombstone, that's all. I feel bad that you died. What happened? Did you get your arm chopped off in an accident or something? Anyway, you don't have to haunt my mom and me anymore. I put your tombstone back, okay? Now please, please leave us alone."

Tim waited as long as he dared for some sign from the ghost. But there wasn't any.

He sighed with relief and fled the cemetery. That night, while Tim and his mother stayed with relatives, a psychic investigator camped out at their apartment and found no further evidence of any ghost.

But Tim already knew that. The ghost of Timothy Murphy — whoever he was — was finally at rest again.

THE HEADLESS TRAINMAN

Keep your eyes peeled and maybe you'll see the Headless Trainman," Chuck Morgan told the kids in his car.

He had just picked up his 12-year-old daughter Allison and her two closest friends, Sasha and Robyn, from the movies and was taking them back to the Morgans' house to spend the night.

In a wind-whipped rainstorm, the car rolled to a stop at a flashing railroad crossing gate on the outskirts of their Tennessee town. "I'm not kidding about the Headless Trainman," he told the girls.

"Oh, Daddy, you're just trying to scare us," said Allison with a smile.

"You shouldn't be so quick to laugh," he said. "It's a legend that's been around here since I was a kid. Many years ago, there was a terrible storm — worse than the one we're having tonight — the one that washed out a section of the tracks down by Daisy Hollow."

"That's not too far from where you live, Allison," interrupted Sasha.

"Anyway," Mr. Morgan continued, "a railroad employee grabbed a lantern and went out to warn an approaching freight train. But he slipped and fell on the tracks and knocked himself out just as the train was coming around the

18

bend. Naturally, the engineer didn't see him and the poor guy was decapitated — you know, his head was cut off."

"Gross," said the girls.

"The train derailed, but fortunately no one else was injured. The strange thing is, ever since the trainman was killed, people have reported seeing a mysterious light swinging back and forth alongside the tracks during bad weather. Legend says it's the ghost of the trainman holding a lantern and looking for his lost head."

"Has anybody seen the ghost recently?" asked Robyn.

"The last I heard, someone spotted him about four or five years ago," said Mr. Morgan.

"Come on, Robyn, you don't really believe that stuff, do you?" Allison said.

"Well, it's possible."

Just then, a bolt of lightning and a thunderous boom made everyone in the car jump. "It's probably the Headless Trainman showing his anger about non-believers," cracked Sasha.

Later that night in Allison's bedroom, with the wind and rain pelting the window, the three girls gossiped for hours about boys and school until they were too tired to talk anymore. As they were drifting off to sleep, they heard a freight train rumbling slowly along the tracks that sliced through the woods half a mile from the Morgans' house.

"You don't suppose the Headless Trainman is out there tonight?" Robyn asked her two friends. "After all, it is a stormy night and —"

"Robyn, go to sleep," moaned Allison, throwing the covers over her head.

A few days later, when the trio was doing homework at the library, Sasha finished her report ahead of the others. To pass the time, she looked in the library's card catalog for local legends about ghosts. To her surprise, she found several references to the trainman — including a copy of an article in the local newspaper dated August 24, 1937.

"Look at this!" she whispered excitedly. "The story of the Headless Trainman is true! See, his name was Willy Wilson, and he was 32 years old when he was hit by the train. Now look at this." She opened up a book about Tennessee ghosts and read the girls a paragraph that talked about people who began seeing a strange swinging light by the tracks on stormy nights.

"First Robyn, now you," said Allison, shaking her head. "Look, if you two are so sure there's a headless ghost out there, then let's go find it and see for ourselves."

The next Saturday night, Allison invited the girls to spend the night. They waited until her parents had fallen asleep before they slipped out of the house into the warm, muggy night. Guided by flashlights, the girls hiked through the woods to the tracks.

"Now what do we do?" asked Robyn.

"I don't know," said Sasha. "I've never been ghost hunting before."

The girls sat by the side of the tracks and began feeling a little scared. Here they were out in the woods . . . alone . . . after midnight.

"Maybe it's time to go back," said Robyn.

"Shhh," whispered Allison. "What's that?"

The girls stood up and peered down the tracks. About 100 yards (91 m) away was a small dancing light heading their way!

"It's the Headless Trainman!" Robyn cried.

She started to run off, but Allison held on to her arm. "Wait, let's get a better look. We'll hide in the bushes as he goes by." The girls scrambled into the brush and crouched down low.

As the swaying light grew closer, the girls could hear footsteps crunching on the gravel. Their hearts started beating faster and faster as the mysterious figure drew nearer. "I'm getting out of here!" said Robyn as she sprang to her feet and ran back into the woods. Sasha and Allison were right behind her.

Then a voice from the tracks yelled out, "Hey, who's out there?" A dog began barking. "Oh, hush, Goldie. It's probably just an old raccoon."

After running through the brush, Allison grabbed the other girls and brought them to a halt. "That was no ghost back there," she said. "That was Old Man Lundvall and his dog."

The girls laughed and giggled all the way back to Allison's house. They quickly forgot all about the Headless Trainman . . . until two months later.

"Did you see the story in the newspaper?" Sasha asked breathlessly as she ran up to Robyn and Allison, who were standing by their school lockers.

"What story?" asked Robyn.

"The Headless Trainman! Some hunters spotted him on the tracks a few days ago! Here, read it yourself."

The girls eagerly pored over the story. It stated that during a late-night rainstorm, two local hunters were hurrying back to their pickup truck when they saw a man holding a lighted lantern running down the tracks. They swear that as he neared them, it looked as though he had no head. Then he disappeared into thin air.

"I think he's real!" declared Sasha.

"I told you he existed!" said Robyn.

"Maybe so, but I want to see him for myself before I

believe it," said Allison.

"We can't keep going out late at night hoping he shows up," said Robyn. "Besides, it gets a little scary out there."

"Maybe one of the reasons we didn't see him was because he only comes out on stormy nights," said Sasha. "We need to wait for the right time."

"Oh, great," said Robyn. "Do we really want to be out there in the rain?"

"It's bound to rain one of these weekends," said Allison. "And when it does, you can spend the night at my house and we'll go from there. But I've got another idea that might help. Why don't we give him a head?"

"What are you talking about?" asked Robyn.

"I get it," said Sasha. "The Headless Trainman is probably out looking for his head. So we'll make him one. . ."

". . . out of papier-mâché and take it with us," Allison added. "Maybe he'll at least want to try it on."

"Try it on?" said Robyn. "You think we're going to walk around with a head in our hands looking for a ghost?"

"Why not?" said Allison. "If nothing else, it'll be fun making the head, and we'll have a story to tell someday. Let's make a promise not to mention this to anyone until after we find him."

Turning to Allison, Robyn said, "I can't believe this is coming from you. You're the one who didn't believe any of this ghost stuff in the first place."

The next weekend, the girls gathered in the basement of Allison's house and went to work making a head for the Headless Trainman. "Do you think he had a big nose?" Robyn asked, laughing.

"I say make him look good," Sasha answered. "Why take a chance?"

The girls painted the head with black hair, blue eyes,

bushy eyebrows, a curled-up mustache, and a big, happy smile. They even managed to top off the head with an old engineer's cap Sasha had found in her attic.

Then came the scariest hours of their lives.

———————

Thundershowers had rolled in late that afternoon and were expected to continue throughout the evening. Allison called her two buddies and crowed, "Tonight's the night. We're going to find us a ghost!"

Around midnight, the girls — dressed in rain gear and carrying flashlights and the head — sneaked out of the Morgans' house and tromped in a light rain through the woods to the tracks in Daisy Hollow. Despite the lousy weather, they were in high spirits, laughing and joking along the way. "Come here, Mr. Trainman. We've got a head for you!"

But after about an hour, the girls were getting tired of their lark. "This has to be the stupidest thing we've ever done," said Robyn.

"Oh, I don't know," said Allison. "What about the time we climbed up the tree outside Buddy McClaren's bedroom window and —"

"You hush up about that," said Robyn. "Just look at us. We're out here in the middle of the night in the rain carrying a papier-mâché head waiting for a headless ghost to show up. Is that stupid or what?"

"It does sound pretty lame," admitted Sasha. "What do you say we head back home?"

As Sasha and Robyn got up from their hiding place in the bushes by the side of the railroad bed, they noticed Allison hadn't joined them. "Allison, aren't you coming with us?" asked Sasha.

23

Allison didn't answer. She was staring at something down the tracks. Through the drizzle she could see a faint, reddish light that grew steadily brighter and larger. It was swaying to and fro above the tracks.

By now, the other girls had spotted it too.

"That's not a flashlight," Sasha whispered with a touch of fear in her voice. "It's flickering — like a lantern."

As the light came closer, the girls stood frozen in terror. They could see the figure of a man in a long cloak holding an old-fashioned railroad lantern. But he wasn't exactly walking. He was floating in the air a few inches above the tracks!

The girls were too petrified to flee. They held their breath and squeezed each other's hands, praying he would ignore them. Then, as he glided past them, they gasped in disbelief. The light from the lantern sent them into shock — because they could plainly see the man had no head!

The terror-stricken girls shrieked in horror and tore through the woods, crashing into bushes and tripping over each other in their panic. They ran and screamed until their lungs felt like they were going to burst. Scratched and bruised from their mad dash, the girls finally scrambled back to the Morgans' house.

"It was him! It was him!" cried Robyn.

"He's out there!" said Allison. "He's really out there!"

"I'll never be able to sleep again as long as I live," said Sasha with a shudder.

After they had calmed down a bit, Sasha asked Allison, "Where's the head we made?"

"I left it back there by the side of the tracks when we started to run. I hope he's got it and likes it because I'm not going to get it. In fact, I'm never going back to Daisy Hollow again — day or night."

24

"Do you think there's any chance our imaginations got carried away, and it was Old Man Lundvall or someone playing a joke on us?" asked Sasha.

"No way," said Allison. "None of us told anyone about what we had planned to do, right? So why would anyone be out there playing a joke? Also, that man had no head, remember? And how do you explain the fact that he was floating above the tracks?"

"Let's not forget we all saw the same thing, so it couldn't have been our imaginations," Robyn added.

A few hours later the girls were still too upset to sleep. So shortly before daybreak, Allison led her friends downstairs for an early breakfast. As she entered the kitchen, she flicked on the light and stopped cold. Sasha bumped into her and said, "Hey, what's up?"

Allison didn't say a word. She was too stunned to speak. With one hand covering her mouth, Allison stepped aside and, with a trembling finger, pointed to the kitchen table. Resting on the table was the papier-mâché head they had made for the Headless Trainman!

But even more shocking was its face. Instead of the warm, friendly smile they had painted on it, the face now sported a sinister scowl!

THE SECRET OF
ROOM 333

If it hadn't been for Sister Cecilia, Adam Bolton never would have passed his math test, never would have gone on the camping trip to the Ozark Mountains — and never would have learned the chilling secret of Room 333.

Adam, a curly-haired sixth grader, attended St. Clare's, a Catholic school in St. Louis that had been around for over 50 years. More than 600 kids crammed into the old three-story brick building. The desks were uncomfortable, the radiators banged in the winter, the window air conditioners rattled on warm days, and the audio-visual equipment often broke down. But St. Clare's still had an excellent reputation for turning out good students, because the teachers truly cared about them.

Adam didn't mind school, especially during basketball and baseball seasons, when he got to show off his athletic skills. He was one of St. Clare's best players. His report card wasn't too bad, either — mostly B's, a few C's, and maybe an A every now and then whenever he really put his mind to it. He would have made the honor roll a couple of times — but his math grades always kept him off it.

For Adam, sixth-grade math was the pits. It was difficult for him to grasp each new chapter. He managed to struggle through the first half of the year — until it came time to study fractions. He just didn't get it.

From then on, Adam dreaded going to math class. Every day was the same in Room 333. His teacher, Miss Townsend, would explain how to multiply and divide fractions, and Adam would get that empty feeling in the pit of his stomach that comes from being totally lost.

But there was something else that bothered him about Room 333. He couldn't put his finger on it, except that he always felt uneasy in there. Maybe it was because that's where math had always been taught. Maybe it was because the rattling window air conditioner sometimes drowned out the teacher's voice. Or maybe it was because Adam had received a D and an F on his last two math exams!

"Adam," said Miss Townsend as she returned the graded quiz from the day before, "can I see you after class?"

One look at his paper and Adam knew why — he had scored a big fat zero, missing all ten of the problems.

When class was dismissed, he went up to Miss Townsend's desk, knowing what she was going to say. "Adam, it's obvious you need help, or you're going to fail this grading period," she told him. "The test is only a week away, which means you have precious little time to learn fractions. Now, if you're willing, I'll give you some extra tutoring. Can you come in after school?"

"I've got baseball practice," said Adam.

"Well, you'll have to decide what's more important. Math or baseball. But remember, if you fail the grading period, you can't play baseball."

"I guess I'll see you this afternoon," he said with a sigh.

Later, in the cafeteria, Adam sat down to lunch with his best friend, Frankie Lewis. "Tell Coach Roberts I'll be half an hour late for practice today," Adam said. "Miss Townsend is going to tutor me."

"That bad, huh?"

"If I flunk math, I'm off the team. And my dad will be furious. Unless I pull at least a C in all my classes, he says the camping trip to the Ozarks is off. The problem is, I just don't get fractions. I don't know whether Miss Townsend goes too fast or what, but I'm lost. She puts that stuff up on the board and expects me to follow it, but I can't."

"I'm in the same boat," said Frankie. "I'm not sure I understand it either."

"At least you passed the quiz."

"Hey, I got lucky — a D. But that could keep me off the honor roll."

"I got shut out," moaned Adam as his head slumped into his hands.

"Hey, speaking of shutouts, did you hear what the Cardinals did to the Dodgers last night?"

When the final bell of the day sounded, Adam trudged into Room 333. He closed the door behind him, sat down at a desk, and waited for Miss Townsend. He gazed out the window, feeling sorry for himself, and listened to the laughter and shouts of kids running to their buses and rides home. *I should be out on the practice field, not here,* he grumbled to himself. *Coach Roberts is going to be mad when I show up late. Where is Miss Townsend anyway?*

"Shouldn't you have your math book open?"

The voice of an elderly woman startled Adam from his thoughts. He was surprised to see a nun by his side. She was dressed in a black robe and hood with a white collar, and had a large gold cross dangling from her neck. Wrinkles spread out from around her big brown eyes and gentle smile. But what Adam noticed most was her snow white skin and rosy cheeks.

"I didn't hear you come in," he said.

28

"I didn't mean to frighten you," she replied. "Nuns have a tendency to do that to children, don't they?"

"Yes, Ma'am, I mean, Sister." He felt a little rattled because he had never actually spoken to a nun who wore the traditional robe, called a habit. Although this was a Catholic school, most of the teachers were not from the clergy. The few nuns and priests who did teach there wore regular clothes.

"Are you having trouble in math?" she asked.

"Fractions," he muttered in disgust. "I think I have a mental block. I get all confused between numerators and denominators, converting and inverting, and —"

"Sounds like you could use a little help," she said. "Mind if I try?"

"I guess so," he answered halfheartedly.

The nun leaned on a desk next to Adam's and proceeded to go over the basics of fractions — material the class had covered weeks earlier but which had left him in a fog. However, she did it in a way that made it more understandable than Adam had thought possible. When he easily managed to solve all ten exercise problems in the book, he thrust his fist up in the air and shouted, "All right!"

"Very good," praised the nun. "Now do a couple more problems and then maybe we can continue tomorrow morning before class."

"Okay," said Adam with a smile. As soon as he knocked off the last two problems, he looked up to thank her for the help. But she was gone.

That's funny, he thought. *She was right next to me just a second ago. How come I didn't see her leave? I didn't hear the door open or close. Boy, those old nuns sure can be quiet.* He glanced up at the clock. *Oh, no! 3:45! I've been here an hour? Coach is going to kill me!*

29

When Adam arrived late for practice, Coach Roberts looked him in the eye and said, "I thought you were going to be only 30 minutes late."

"I'm having trouble with fractions," Adam said with a sheepish grin. "It took longer than I thought."

"Fractions, huh? I had trouble too, when I was your age," Coach Roberts said with a wink. "Now get out there at third base!"

After practice, Adam hustled over to Frankie and happily told him, "I think I've finally figured out how to multiply fractions!"

"What happened? Did you get a new brain?"

"Real funny. No, this old nun — I've never seen her before — showed up, and it was like she turned on a light inside my head. All of a sudden I understood how to do the problems."

"So do you think you can pass the big test?" asked Frankie.

"I hope so. But I still have to learn how to divide fractions."

"That's my big hang-up," said Frankie. "It has me stumped. Do you think she could help me too?"

"I'm going to see her tomorrow morning before school. Why don't you come with me?"

Before first period the next morning, the boys entered the empty classroom, sat in the front row, and waited for the nun. Moments later, from the back of the room came a voice. "Ready to learn how to divide fractions?" The boys spun in their seats and saw the old nun standing in the back corner. Then they turned around and stared at the only door in the room, which was located in the front. It was still closed.

"We didn't see you come in," said Adam. "Have you

been there the whole time?"

"In a manner of speaking, yes," she answered.

A surprised Frankie whispered to Adam, "How did she do that?"

Adam just shook his head in bewilderment. "Uh, Sister, this is my friend Frankie, and he's having trouble dividing fractions too."

"Well then, let's get right to it," she said. For the next half hour, the nun tutored the boys until they finally caught on. As they worked on the last exercise problem, the classroom door swung open and Miss Townsend walked in.

"Adam, I owe you an apology," she said, putting her briefcase on her desk. "I had to leave school early yesterday because my daughter hurt her arm on the swing set at the day care center. I had to take her to the doctor. She's okay. But I'm sorry I forgot to leave you a note. I hope you didn't wait too long for me. I promise I'll help you after school today."

"That's okay, Ma'am," said Adam. "I understand how to multiply and divide fractions. Sister here helped me."

"Sister? Who are you talking about?"

"Her." Adam pointed to the desk next to his, and his mouth dropped open. The nun had disappeared. "The nun. You know, the nun who was here just a second ago. You had to have seen her when you came in."

"Frankie, do you know what he's talking about?" asked the teacher.

"Honest, Miss Townsend, there was an old nun in a black robe like from the old days, and she was helping us with our fractions when you walked in."

The teacher shook her head and smiled in a way that left the boys convinced she didn't believe them. "But we

31

don't have nuns in habits in this school. I don't know what kind of joke you're trying to pull, but I'll be here after class if you need me, okay?"

As the boys left the room, they didn't know what to think. "One minute she's there, the next minute she's gone," muttered Adam.

"How did she do that?" Frankie wondered.

On the day of the big test, butterflies were fluttering in Adam's stomach. "I've got an awful lot riding on this," he told Frankie. "I need a decent grade, or it's bye-bye to baseball and the Ozarks."

"Yeah, and I'll blow my chance to make the honor roll if I mess up. But like Sister told us, relax, take a deep breath, and think positively."

That's exactly what the boys did when they began the test. With each problem, Adam's confidence grew. *I know how to do it!* he thought. *Yes! Piece of cake!*

Meanwhile, Frankie was breezing through the exam too. About halfway through, both boys felt a strange urge to look up from their tests at the same time. And there, in the front of the room, stood the old nun. She smiled at them and then motioned for them to get back to work.

"Boys, keep your heads down!" warned Miss Townsend.

"We were just looking at the, uh. . . ." Adam's voice trailed off when he realized the nun had vanished again.

". . . the clock, Miss Townsend," added Frankie. "We were just looking at the clock to see how much time we had left."

As they left the classroom, Adam turned to Frankie and said, "Do you believe that nun? How could she sneak in and out without anyone seeing her? Is she playing a game with us?"

"Beats me," Frankie said. "All I know is I think I aced the test!"

Adam grinned. "I think I nailed it too."

A few days later, the boys got the news — A's for both of them!

"Yesssss!" shouted Frankie. "I'm headed for the honor roll again!" He high-fived Adam, who hollered, "Ozarks, here I come!"

After whooping it up, the boys decided to track down the nun and thank her for tutoring them. So they walked into the administration office and asked the secretary, Mrs. Painter, to help them.

"What's her name?" she asked.

"Gee, we don't know," said Adam.

"Well, can you describe her?"

"She was in her sixties I guess," said Adam. "She was short like you, Mrs. Painter. And, well, she was on the heavy side."

"She was fat," added Frankie, "but not like you, Mrs. Painter."

"She had these big brown eyes and the whitest skin I've ever seen, and really rosy cheeks," said Adam. "And she wore a black robe that old nuns used to wear."

"I've been at St. Clare's for eight years, and I don't know of anyone who's ever fit that description — with or without the habit," said Mrs. Painter. "And there haven't been any nuns visiting us lately who wear habits. I'm sorry, but I can't help you."

As the perplexed boys were about to leave the office, Dwight, the janitor who had been a fixture at the school for years, stopped working on the thermostat and said, "Excuse me, boys. I couldn't help but overhear you. Did you happen to see this nun in Room 333?"

"Yes," said Adam excitedly. "Do you know her?"

"Sounds like Sister Cecilia. She taught at St. Clare's for about 30 years — most of that time right in Room 333. She was a great teacher. It didn't matter what grade she taught, she had a knack for making math easy for most everyone. In fact, she took pride in knowing that no one — not one single student — ever flunked her class."

"She sure helped us out," said Adam. "So where can we find her? We want to thank her."

Dwight leaned on the wall and chuckled. "Now, boys, you're going to find this hard to believe. But Sister Cecilia died about ten years ago. She had a heart attack right in that very same room."

"Whoa, hold on," said Adam. "She can't be dead. We saw her. We heard her. She helped us."

"You know, every few years since her death, I hear about a student or two getting help from her," said Dwight.

"Are you saying she's a ghost?" asked Frankie in disbelief.

"You're the ones who saw her, not me," said Dwight. "All I'm saying is you described Sister Cecilia, and she's been dead for about ten years."

"That's incredible!" said Adam. "Could it be possible a ghost helped me ace a test?"

"Hey," added Frankie, "I can handle that." He looked up toward the ceiling and said, "Thanks, Sister Cecilia, wherever you are."

THE HOME WRECKER

Jenny Clark didn't mean to invite a real ghost into her house. She just wanted to inject some fun into her slumber party by holding a seance.

She and her girlfriends sat in a circle around a candle late at night, held hands, and hoped to summon the spirit of her dead grandmother, or a murder victim, or maybe even someone famous like Amelia Earhart.

It was all for fun because Jenny didn't believe in ghosts. That is, until she and her parents experienced two horrifying nights of sheer terror.

———————

Jenny, a perky 13-year-old with straight dark hair that fell to her waist, lived with her parents in a small Oregon town. Her father, Jim, worked in a hardware store and her mother, Marsha, did volunteer work as a teacher's aide.

Jenny, a talkative teen with a vivid imagination, always threw great slumber parties. So when she invited four of her junior-high friends — Amy, Renee, Jodi, and Barbara — for an overnight, they were psyched for a good time.

As they gathered in her bedroom, Jenny announced with dramatic flair, "Tonight we are going to step where people fear to tread — into the unknown, into the world of the beyond." Squinting her pretty blue eyes and talking in a hushed tone, she told her friends, "Tonight, we're going to invite a ghost to spend the night with us."

The girls giggled — a few nervously — as Jenny put them into the proper mood for chills and thrills. "The power of the mind is very strong," she said. "If we concentrate hard enough, we could attract a ghost to come into the room. But we should do a mind exercise first. If we put all our energy together, four of us can lift Amy with just two fingers on each hand."

"No way," said Amy, who weighed about 110 pounds.

"I'll prove it," Jenny declared. With Amy lying prone and rigid on the floor, the other girls kneeled around her — one at her feet, another by her head, and one on each side of her. They had to tell themselves Amy wasn't heavy. Then repeatedly chanting, "Light as a feather, stiff as a board . . . light as a feather, stiff as a board," the girls slowly began to lift her with their fingers! Amy was almost two feet (.6 m) above the floor before Renee became so freaked out that she screamed, breaking their concentration. Amy fell to the floor with a thud, and everyone burst out laughing.

Jenny didn't know it yet, but she was about to unlock an invisible door to the unknown — with terrifying results.

She rummaged around in her closet and brought out an old Ouija® board, a device that some people believe can receive messages from beyond this world. "Let's ask the Mystifying Oracle some questions, okay?" said Jenny.

The girls gathered around the board, and Jenny and Renee placed their fingers lightly on the message indicator. For more than an hour, as the girls concentrated, the indicator moved across the board seemingly by itself. I. answered questions by pointing to the "yes" or "no" marked on the board and to letters on the board, which spelled out words.

The Ouija® board told the girls that Brandon had a crush on Jenny, Renee's parents would not get divorced, Amy would marry Mike and have four kids, Jodi would make the basketball team, and Barbara would ace the big science test.

Then Jenny asked the Ouija® board if there was a spirit in the room. The girls shuddered when it answered "yes." She asked for the spirit's name, and it spelled out Z-E-B-Y-N. "Zebyn?" said Jenny. "What kind of name is that? Ouija, who is Zebyn?" The indicator didn't answer. Instead, it spelled "B-Y-E."

"It's almost midnight and now comes the real fun," said Jenny. "We're going to hold a seance!"

She brought out a fat candle, lit it, set it on the floor, and turned off the lights. Then the girls sat in a circle around the candle and held hands. "Now concentrate," Jenny whispered. "Let your minds open up . . . reach out to the beyond . . . let us invite someone from the spirit world to come forth and make his or her presence felt. Zebyn, are you out there? Make yourself known to us."

But Zebyn failed to materialize, so the girls called on the spirits of dead grandmothers, uncles, and even a family dog. They tried to make contact with everyone from President John F. Kennedy to Joan of Arc. But there were no signs of any ghost. Until. . . .

"Do you smell something?" Jenny asked.

"It's like flowers or something," Renee replied. "And it's getting stronger."

The fragrance soon became almost sickening. "You know what this reminds me of?" said Amy. "A funeral home. I was at my uncle's wake last week, and there were tons of flowers there. But this smell is so much stronger."

"I wonder where it's coming from," said Jenny. "Did one

37

of you open a bottle of perfume?" All the girls shook their heads, and a search of the bedroom turned up nothing.

They opened the windows and let the nippy November breeze clear the air. But then the girls were assaulted with a new smell — a disgusting odor of rotten eggs so foul it left them gagging and forced them from the bedroom.

The horrible stench followed them down the hall and into the living room, where Jenny's parents already were rushing to open the windows. Mr. and Mrs. Clark and the girls conducted a careful check of the house, but failed to find where the putrid smell was coming from.

"I wonder if some kids — friends of yours at school — hit the house with a stink bomb," said Jim after the stench had gone away. "If I find out who they are, they're in big trouble." Looking at his watch, he added, "It's almost 1:00 in the morning, girls. Let's all go to bed now. And tomorrow, Jenny, tell your friends I didn't find their prank funny at all."

Sitting at the desk in her bedroom the following night, Jenny was doing her homework when she was jolted by a loud banging noise coming from inside the wall At first she thought her dad was fixing something.

"What's all that pounding?" shouted her father from the living room.

"It's not me, Daddy," answered Jenny. "I thought you were doing it." As her dad walked into her room, the banging stopped. But then it started again from inside another wall. Bam! Bam! Bam! It sounded like a giant hammer. A minute later, the pounding moved to the ceiling, then to another wall, and finally to the floor. Then it stopped.

The bizarre odors and banging upset Jenny so much that she got her sleeping bag and slept on the floor in her parents' room. But what had happened up to now was

38

nothing compared to the terror they would experience the following night.

———

Jenny was in the living room watching TV with her parents when their house came alive as if it had a mind — a very mean one — of its own.

While the Clarks were watching a rerun of "Cheers," their television set suddenly toppled over. As the three leaped to their feet, two framed pictures on the living room wall crashed onto the floor. But the pictures didn't just slip off their hooks and slide down the wall. They flew off and landed near the opposite side of the room as if some invisible force had yanked them off their hooks and flung them. Jenny and her parents were still in shock, trying to figure out what was happening to them, when a lamp shot straight up to the ceiling, smashing into bits.

"Jenny! Marsha! Get out of the house! Now!" shouted Jim as he grabbed his wife and daughter and hustled them out onto the lawn. Behind them, the family could still hear sounds of objects crashing and smashing inside.

"Daddy, what's happening?" cried Jenny.

"I don't know," said Jim. "Maybe an earthquake or something." But when he looked around, he noticed that no one else in the neighborhood had rushed outside. Besides, the ground wasn't shaking. When the racket died down about a minute later, Jim cautiously walked back into the house and moaned, "This is unbelievable!" Jenny and her mother ran inside and were sickened by the sight.

The living room looked like a battle scene. Every picture on the wall had been smashed. The couch was overturned, and the two easy chairs had been flipped on their backs and tossed in a corner. An end table had been smashed. All the drawers of the hutch had been pulled out and the contents dumped. Part of the table lamp was sticking in a wall.

Sobbing and near hysterics, Jenny raced out of the house and pounded on the door of their next-door neighbor, police officer Tony Hudson. "Help us!" she yelled. "Strange things are happening in our house! Awful, terrible things!"

Officer Hudson dashed over to the Clarks' house and couldn't believe his eyes when he saw the destruction in the living room.

"Who did this?" he asked. "Do you know who ransacked your house?"

"It's not a question of who did this, Tony," said Jim. "I think it's more like what did this. We were here the whole time when suddenly everything started flying around the room — all by themselves — and crashing right before our eyes."

Trembling and feeling faint, Jenny walked into the kitchen for a glass of water only to shriek in terror. Drawers began opening and slamming shut by themselves before they shot out of the cabinets and dumped knives, forks, and spoons onto the floor. Then the shelves in the cupboards started vibrating until dishes and glasses tumbled out. Jenny frantically tried to catch the falling china and glassware, but most of the breakables crashed to the floor.

By now, her startled parents and Officer Hudson were standing in shock in the kitchen doorway. While they were still trying to understand what they were witnessing, the refrigerator slowly lifted about six inches off the floor, tilted to the left, and then set back down with a clunk.

Officer Hudson immediately called for the police. When four officers arrived, they were stunned by the mess inside. But whatever strange force was at work had stopped. The Clarks explained what had happened, but the police weren't ready to buy their incredible story. The officers examined the house thoroughly, looking for any kind of logical explanation, but couldn't come up with one.

Meanwhile, Jenny fearfully walked down the hall and peeked inside her bedroom — and screamed. Everyone rushed to the doorway and saw the books on her shelf fall one by one onto the floor. Then her desk chair rose by itself, did a flip, and landed on the bed.

"I don't believe this," said one of the officers. "How am I going to write up what I just saw in my report? This is crazy. I can't even begin to explain it."

The emotionally drained family spent the night next door with the Hudsons and woke up in the morning to see a story splashed on the front page of the local newspaper with the headline: "Police Say House Is Haunted."

When the Clarks returned to their home, there was no evidence that anything else had occurred during the night. When a follow-up police investigation failed to find any clue to the baffling mystery, a city engineer was called in to examine the structure of the house. He couldn't find anything wrong.

After helping to clean up the mess, Jenny was still too scared to sleep at home. So she stayed with the Hudsons while her parents bravely spent the night in their own home.

Although the Clarks experienced no ghostly incidents, there was one scary moment. About 3:00 A.M., Jenny tossed and turned and suddenly sat up in bed. She had an uneasy feeling that something bad was happening. She gazed out the window across the yard and spotted a man with a can in his hand, sprinkling something around her house. She ran from her room and woke up Officer Hudson.

While she called her parents to alert them, the officer grabbed his gun and ran outside. He discovered two men and a woman lurking around the Clark house. "Police!" he shouted. "Freeze!"

As he stepped toward them, the woman hissed, "There is an evil spirit in there. It must be burned." After calling for backup, Officer Hudson discovered that the three prowlers had poured gasoline around the house and were about to set it on fire! The three people were arrested after admitting they tried to burn down the house to get rid of the ghost.

"The fire might not have gotten rid of the evil spirit," said Jim later, "but it certainly would have gotten rid of us."

Jenny was a nervous wreck and felt even worse when the newspaper ran another front-page story the next day: "Haunted House a Hoax, Says Police Chief." In the article, the police chief denied that a ghost had invaded the Clark house.

Instead, he placed the blame squarely on the shoulders of Jenny! "The only time these objects supposedly flew through the air was when Jenny Clark was in the room," he said. "Nothing ever happened when she wasn't there."

Jenny tossed the paper down and burst into tears. "It's not true! I didn't do it!" She buried her head in her mother's shoulder and sobbed. "How could I? How can a 95-pound (43-kg) girl move a refrigerator? You were there, and so were the police. We all saw things flying around. I couldn't have done it."

"We know, honey, we know," said her mother, stroking Jenny's hair. "Officer Hudson told me that all the police officers who were here know you couldn't have done it. He

42

also said the police chief told his officers he would suspend them if they said anything publicly about a ghost. They told him the truth, but he didn't care. He just wanted someone to blame because he doesn't want to scare people into thinking there's a ghost loose in the neighborhood."

The phone rang and Jenny answered it. "Hey, Jenny," said Kyle, a boy from her class. "I read the story in the paper this morning. Do me a favor, okay? I've got a bet with James. Tell me, how did you do it? Did you use wires or what?"

Jenny slammed the receiver down and started to cry again. "I can never show my face in school again! Everyone will make fun of me. I can't stand to live here anymore. Oh, Mom, what am I going to do?"

Later that morning, Mark Warner, an investigator of unexplained phenomena, visited the Clarks at the suggestion of Officer Hudson. Warner interviewed Jim and Marsha and examined the house. He then talked with Jenny, who described in detail everything she had seen. She pointed out where she had stood in each room when the objects began their baffling flights of destruction.

"Now, you said all these weird things started happening a couple of nights ago, right?" Warner asked.

"The only thing that happened the first night was those yucky smells," said Jenny.

"What were you doing before those odors came?"

"I was having a slumber party. We were playing with the Ouija® board, and then we held a —" She gasped. "We held a seance, and I was trying to get a ghost to appear. I mean I was, but I wasn't. I was just fooling around trying to scare everyone because, you know, there aren't any such things as ghosts. At least I didn't think there were."

43

"What we probably have here is a case of poltergeist activity," said Warner. "A poltergeist is a nasty ghost that likes to cause trouble. It comes from some kind of psychic energy it picks up from a person or persons in the house. I know you didn't do the things the police chief says you did. However, I suspect you may have been the cause."

"Me? But how?" asked Jenny in disbelief.

"Well, there have been cases where poltergeists make their presence felt only after they've been invited from the spirit world into our own world, like holding a seance or by merely asking it to come forth."

"But I was just joking."

"It looks like the joke was on you — and a pretty bad one at that."

"This poltergeist, is it Zebyn, the one the Ouija® board said was in my room?"

"I don't know," said Warner. "The Ouija® board has no power of its own. It's just a way of getting you in tune with psychic energy much like a candle or music or a book can get you in the right mood. Whatever is out there is some force that has attached itself to you."

"How do we make it go away?" asked Jenny.

"There's one thing we could try and hope that it works — hold another seance."

After much convincing, Jenny's four friends from her slumber party reluctantly returned to the house later that evening. The girls, along with Warner, gathered in a circle around the same lit candle and held hands. "Please, Zebyn, if that's your name, go back to where you came from and leave us alone," pleaded Jenny. "I didn't mean to invite you. You don't belong here. Now go and leave us alone!"

Suddenly, the walls in the room shook with three loud

44

bangs, and then the candle flickered and went out. The girls screamed and ran out of the room in a panic.

But to the everyone's relief, the house remained quiet. No banging walls, no flying objects, no sickening smells.

"I think he's gone for good," declared Warner.

Nothing bizarre ever happened again in the house — except for one blood-chilling moment the next night, which was the first time Jenny tried sleeping in her own room again. She had just turned off the light and was about to go to sleep when she noticed a faint flickering glow in the room. Jenny raised her head, and her heart leaped into her throat. The candle — the very same one used in the seance — had suddenly lit up on its own!

THE GHOST OF
SLOW SAM

Twelve-year-old Danny Reese prided himself on being as brave as any boy he knew. So when his buddy, Gerry "Bo" Young, dared him to spend the night in an old cemetery with him, he readily agreed.

It was the scariest thing he ever did.

Danny and Bo were members of a Boy Scout troop of 24 members. They were spending a week at summer camp in a park a few hours from their Atlanta home. On the third day of their camp out, the troop was taking an evening hike down a seldom-used dirt road.

The sun had already set behind a stand of magnolia trees when the Scouts came across an old cemetery on the gentle slope of a small hill. About 100 moss-covered gravestones about a foot high stood in neat rows. As the boys explored the cemetery, they noticed that the names carved into the markers were hard to read. But those stones that were legible all bore the same date of death — November 19, 1864.

"This is a graveyard from the Civil War," explained Scoutmaster Trent Manson. "When General William T. Sherman of the Union Army was leading his men to Savannah after sacking Atlanta, there was a bloody battle with the Confederate Army near here. The rebel soldiers who lost their lives in that fight were buried here."

46

Mr. Manson looked at his watch and then said, "We can only spend a few more minutes here because it's starting to get dark. We have a 30-minute walk back to our campsite."

When the boys left the graveyard, the first stars of the night had made their appearance, and the crickets, frogs, and birds had struck up their evening concert. Then something really strange happened. Something very spooky.

The night suddenly became absolutely quiet. Nature's chorus of chirps, croaks, and warbles had stopped unexpectedly. Bo was the first to notice. "How come it got so quiet all of a sudden?" he asked. A cold chill seemed to descend on the boys from out of nowhere. By now all the scouts had come to a halt.

"Look, over there!" someone shouted. They all wheeled to the right. A few hundred feet away, a faint mist began to curl its way through some dogwood trees. It grew bigger and brighter, turning from a pale gray to a shiny, yellowish glow. As the boys watched in awe, the mist began to take on the fuzzy shape of a person! The boys had to use their imagination to make out the head, body, arms, and legs — much like the shapes that can sometimes be seen in clouds.

Slowly, the eerie mist began to fade away. It turned into a shapeless wisp of smoke and disappeared.

The bewildered scouts turned to each other in nervous laughter and wondered what it was they had just witnessed. Each boy had his own explanation. "It was an alien being beamed up to his UFO" . . . "A mirage" . . . "It's some guy trying to play a joke on us" . . . "Swamp gas" . . . "No, a ghost!" . . . "What do you think it was, Mr. Manson?"

The scoutmaster was dumbfounded. "I-I-I don't know," he stammered, shaking his head as he continued to stare into the woods. "I simply don't know. It was probably some kind

47

of oddity — like maybe a hunter is out there with a flashlight, and it reflected his image off the mist, or something like that." He could tell his troop wasn't buying that explanation. In fact, Mr. Manson didn't believe it himself. "Okay, guys, come on. It's getting late. Let's get back to camp."

That night, after Danny and Bo slipped into their sleeping bags inside their two-man tent, Bo said, "I don't believe in ghosts, do you?"

"Of course not," replied Danny. "That's a bunch of baloney."

"So you're not afraid of ghosts then, right?"

"Of course, not. They don't exist."

"Then I dare you to spend the night in that cemetery back there," Bo challenged.

"Oh, come on, let's get some sleep."

"What's the matter? Are you chicken?"

"No. I just don't see any reason to go. Besides, we could get in trouble for leaving the campgrounds."

"You're afraid, admit it."

"I am not!" snapped Danny. "You want to go to the cemetery, fine. Let's go. We'll see who chickens out first."

With their flashlights leading the way, the two scouts walked back to the cemetery. When they reached the spot where they had seen the ghostly image, Danny had to admit to himself that he was a little spooked. He really didn't want to be out there at all, but Bo dared him. And he wasn't about to back down from a dare. Call him anything, but don't call him chicken.

When they reached the graveyard, Danny wanted to sit by a tree off to the side. "No way," said Bo. "We've got to be right in the middle of the cemetery. And it's got to be right over a grave."

Reluctantly, Danny sat down with his back resting on

48

a marker while Bo did the same thing on another grave-stone facing him.

Danny was starting to sweat, mostly from the warm, muggy air but also because he felt more than a little bit uneasy. He had camped out many times before with his dad and other scouts without any concerns. But this was different. This was in a cemetery.

Although Bo wasn't about to admit it, he was some-what scared too. But since it was his idea, he couldn't exactly call the whole thing off now. Danny would gleeful-ly tell all the others who was really the chicken. No, he'd stick it out and try to outlast his friend.

To mask their fear, the two boys kept talking about anything and everything from baseball to movies to girls. While they were talking, Danny was idly pawing at the ground, digging a little hole with his fingers until it was deep enough to stick his entire hand in.

"Ouch!" he yelped. "I just cut my middle finger on something sharp." With Bo holding a flashlight, Danny dug around the object in the hole. A minute later, he gave a low whistle. "Wow, will you look at this!"

Danny pulled out an old knife with a slightly decayed wooden handle and a slender rusty blade that was broken halfway down the curved shaft. Carved into the handle was either the number "54" or the initials "SH." The boys couldn't quite make it out.

"Do you suppose it's from the Civil War?" Danny asked excitedly. "Man, what a find! Maybe it was used in the battle here. Maybe it was used to kill a soldier."

Danny was blabbering about all the possibilities of who owned the knife and how it got there when Bo inter-rupted him.

"Uh, Danny, do you get the feeling we're not alone?

Like there's someone out there watching us?"

"Knock it off, Bo. If you're tying to scare me, it won't work."

"I'm not. Just listen."

After about ten seconds of silence, Danny said, "I don't hear anything."

"That's the point. There is no sound. All of a sudden, we don't hear any birds or insects or anything. Just like earlier tonight."

As the words tumbled out of Bo's mouth, the boys felt a weird chill. The hair on the backs of their necks stood straight up and goose bumps prickled their arms.

"What do you think?" Bo whispered with alarm.

"Maybe we should head back," said Danny, his throat now feeling uncomfortably dry. "I'm really tired."

"I knew you'd chicken out," sneered Bo, putting on a brave front.

"If you're not going, then I'm not going. I'll stay right here and —" Danny stopped in mid-sentence and slowly stood up to get a better look. "Uh-oh."

From one end of the cemetery the same glowing mist they had seen earlier began to materialize into a human figure. But instead of fading away like before, it began to reveal features. The startled boys could plainly see it was a man in the tattered gray uniform of the Confederate Army! A floppy, torn cavalry hat covered part of his gaunt, unshaven face. His thin lips were curled in a sneer.

The man began to move toward them, slowly and awkwardly. He walked with a terrible limp — his right leg stiff and out to the side as he dragged his right foot. Extending his left arm, he opened his trembling hand with the palm up as if he wanted something from them.

The boys didn't stick around to find out what it was.

Danny and Bo tore out of there as fast as their legs could carry them. Although Danny had always outraced Bo in the past, this time Bo was out in front. Their arms, legs, and hearts kept pumping faster and faster as they ran all the way back to the camp. The boys then dove into their tent and crawled inside their sleeping bags.

While trying to catch his breath, Bo stammered, "I think . . . we saw . . . an honest-to-goodness . . . real-life ghost! I don't know . . . what else . . . it could have been."

"We should tell Mr. Manson," said Danny.

"Yeah, but if we do, we could get into trouble. You know the rule: No leaving the camping area after dark."

"I guess you're right." Just then Danny realized he was still clutching the broken knife in his hand. His fingers were wrapped so tightly around the handle he almost had to pry them off it. As he rested the knife on his backpack by the head of his sleeping bag, he couldn't help but notice that his hands were still shaking.

The boys kept taking deep breaths, trying to relax, but they were much too charged up to sleep. So they began talking again about anything other than ghosts just to keep their minds off the terror they had experienced.

Then it happened again. The tent became enveloped in that same foreboding chill they had felt twice before. "Oh, n-o-o-o-!" moaned Danny. "Please, not again!"

Right before their eyes, the Confederate ghost slowly came into view — inside their tent! He appeared between the two stunned boys, kneeling on his left leg with his right leg angled off to the side of him. First, he glared at Danny and then at Bo. His piercing eyes flashed with anger. Then his hand moved menacingly towards Danny, who quivered helplessly in his sleeping bag.

"He's going to strangle me!" Danny shrieked. But the

51

soldier reached across the terrified boy's head and grabbed the old broken knife. He held it up high over Danny's wildly beating heart. "He's going to stab me!" Danny cried.

Without making a sound or changing his expression, the ghostly soldier rose with great effort, turned around, and disappeared.

The boys were too frightened to move at first. They couldn't believe their eyes. Finally, Bo timidly crawled out of his sleeping bag and peeked outside. "He's gone. There's no sign of him."

The boys were so shaken they stayed awake the rest of the night. That morning, they made a pact not to tell anyone about the ghost for fear of being ridiculed. The next night, while the troop was sitting around the campfire, a local park ranger strolled by and joined them for some idle chat.

Eventually Mr. Manson told the ranger about the bizarre, wispy figure they had seen by the old cemetery the previous night.

The ranger chuckled knowingly. "Well, let me tell you about that. For about 100 years, people have reported seeing some strange things around here — like either a glowing mist or an old rebel soldier. In fact, they have a pretty good idea of what it is. It's the ghost of Slow Sam.

"Sam was a 13-year-old apprentice in a tannery over in Clinton a few miles from here when the War Between the States broke out in 1861. He helped the Confederate cause by supplying troops with leather goods, repairing saddles, and rustling up food and fodder from surrounding farms and plantations.

"When he was 16, he joined the militia and fought in north Georgia and Tennessee. He was badly wounded when he was shot in the right leg, so Sam returned home on leave. He arrived just as more than 2,000 Union troops were advancing on the town. Sam joined his fellow soldiers in a pitched battle right in this area to defend Clinton. The Confederates fought valiantly, but they were outmanned and outgunned by the Yanks, who quickly overran the town. It got pretty ugly. Sam and the others had to stand by helplessly and watch the Union soldiers steal food and supplies from all the merchants and burn down their stores.

"Meanwhile, the battle left about 100 Confederate soldiers dead, and they were buried back there in that cemetery. Now you can understand why Sam had a major hatred for those men in blue.

"When the war was over, Slow Sam — they called him that because he had a terrible limp — still wore his tattered Confederate uniform and his torn cavalry hat. And every chance he got, he cursed the Yankees for what they did to Clinton and the South.

"He went back to tanning hide. But for years after, he tended to the cemetery in his free time and sometimes roamed the old battlefield like he was in a daze, reliving each and every one of those deaths.

"One day, in the 1890's, when he was about 45 years old, Slow Sam came across a man who was poking around the ground with a metal rod near the graveyard. Every so often, the stranger would find something and put it in a leather sack he had slung over his shoulder. Slow Sam struck up a conversation with the man — I think his name was Conway — and learned he was a former Union soldier who had fought in that battle back in 1864. And now here he was hunting for souvenirs to sell.

"Well, you can imagine how that made Slow Sam feel. His old hatred flared up again, and the two got into a heated argument. One thing led to another, and Slow Sam pulled out a long curved tanning knife of his and stabbed Conway right in the ribs. Slow Sam struck him so hard that the blade broke off and stayed stuck right in Conway's side."

Danny and Bo were in shock. It all added up — the man in the tattered Confederate uniform . . . the awful limp. . . and the broken knife. Could it really have been Slow Sam? Then Danny remembered the carving on the handle, "SH."

"Excuse me, sir," said Danny. "Would you happen to know what Slow Sam's last name was?"

"I'm not sure," said the ranger. "Oh, that's right. It was Hartigan — Sam Hartigan. I remember because he was a distant cousin to my great, great aunt."

There was no doubt about it now. Danny and Bo had seen the ghost of Slow Sam. They felt relieved to know they weren't going crazy, that what had happened to them was real. But they also felt scared out of their wits for the same reason.

"No one actually saw the fight," the ranger continued. "So no charges were filed against Slow Sam. But everyone in town figured it was him. The Conway family from up in Ohio wanted Slow Sam arrested. The sheriff was pretty well convinced he did it, but no one ever found the rest of the knife to link it to him. But it didn't matter. Slow Sam died a year later from pneumonia.

"Ever since then, people have reported seeing some crazy mist. Others claim they've actually seen a strange figure limping around the graveyard late at night. Either way, they just assume it's Slow Sam.

"Now, I don't mean to scare you or anything, because personally I think it's all a lot of poppycock. It's just an old legend."

"Yeah," Bo whispered to Danny, "it's a legend all right." Both boys nodded to each other and then said together, "Not!"

THE BABY-SITTING GHOST

Kay Linquist loved to baby-sit. The bubbly 14-year-old was one of the most popular sitters in her neighborhood. Kay loved to get down on the floor with the toddlers and play games and read them bedtime stories. And if the kids were extra good, she'd let them stay up an extra half hour — as long as they didn't tell their parents.

Every baby-sitting job was pretty much the same — pleasant and uneventful. That is, until the night she went to sit for Mr. and Mrs. Tom and Anna Ward, who lived a couple of blocks away. Kay was a last-minute replacement for their regular sitter, an older teenager who was sick. The Wards were a little concerned because it would be the first time they had ever left their six-month-old son Chad in the care of such a young sitter.

After showing Kay the baby's room, where Chad was sleeping peacefully in his crib, Mrs. Ward said, "We'll be home pretty late because we'll be at the theater and then at a party afterwards. Here are the phone numbers of where we'll be as well as the number for the doctor and our next-door neighbor if there are any problems."

"There's no need to worry, Mrs. Ward," said Kay. "I'm an experienced sitter, and besides, if there's a problem my mother is only a few minutes away."

"Chad has had his bottle and should sleep through the

night," said Mrs. Ward. "Help yourself to anything in the refrigerator if you get hungry. We'll call you after the show. Good-bye. And, Kay, don't let anyone in."

When the Wards left, Kay locked the front door and checked the windows and back door to make sure they were secure too. Then, like most sitters in a new house, she took a quick tour of the home. It was a small one-story house with a living room, dining room, kitchen, two bedrooms, and one bath — a typical house in that neighborhood.

Kay plopped down on the couch and turned on the TV with the remote control. To her dismay, the Wards didn't have cable. *Well, this is going to be a boring night,* she thought.

It was going to be a night she would never forget.

From time to time, Kay checked in on the baby, who continued to sleep peacefully. Around 11:30 P.M., Mrs. Ward called and Kay assured her everything was fine. With nothing worth watching on television, Kay picked up a magazine and began reading. The house was very quiet. Her eyelids kept getting heavier, and she soon fell asleep.

Suddenly Kay awoke with a jolt. As her eyes began to focus, her heart almost leaped into her throat. Standing over her was a tall, elderly woman with her hair tied up in a neat bun. She was wearing a white blouse with a lace collar under a dark blue suit. There was something very strange about her, but Kay didn't know what it was. Her skin was very pale, her forehead was lined with deep wrinkles, and her eyes were wide with worry.

"Who-who are you?" Kay stammered.

"Come! Come!" urged the old woman. "It's Chad!"

Kay leaped off the couch, dashed into the nursery, and flipped on the light. The baby was gasping and turning blue. "He's choking to death!" cried Kay. "Help me!" She turned around, but the woman had vanished.

For a brief moment Kay felt paralyzed. Her mind went blank. All her previous baby-sitting experience and all the training she had taken in first-aid class suddenly meant nothing.

Chad's face was turning a darker shade of blue. *Think, Kay, think*, the sitter told herself. *Don't panic!*

Just then she noticed that the old woman had reappeared and was now by her side. "Rest his stomach on your left arm so his head is hanging down," the woman instructed Kay. "There's something stuck in his throat. Reach inside and get it out."

Kay did as she was told and pulled out of the baby's mouth a small gold locket without a chain. Chad gurgled, coughed, and then started to cry. No wailing had ever sounded so good to Kay. As she comforted the baby and held him tightly in her arms, Kay breathed a huge sigh of relief and turned to thank the old woman. But once again, she had disappeared.

After Chad had calmed down and gone back to sleep, Kay tiptoed out of the nursery and into the living room. Her heart was still pounding, and her hands were trembling from Chad's brush with death.

Who was the old woman? Where had she come from? Kay didn't remember hearing any doors open or close. She then checked the front and back doors. They were still locked from the inside, and the windows were secure too. She walked into every room, but there was no sign that anyone else had been in the house.

Was this all a bad dream? Kay wondered. *Was I imagin-*

ing the old woman? She went back into the nursery where Chad was sound asleep. *Maybe none of this happened. Maybe it was just a dream. But it sure seemed real.*

Just as Kay had convinced herself that it was a nightmare, she remembered the locket she had pulled out of Chad's throat. It was sitting on top of the baby's dresser, right where she had left it. *This was no dream, that's for sure.*

She walked back into the living room, holding the locket. *I wonder if there's anything inside of it.* Slowly she opened it up and was stunned by what she saw. Inside was a tiny photo of the old woman!

A short while later, the Wards came home. Kay told them everything that had happened. Well, almost everything. She left out the part about the old woman. When Kay finished her account, Mrs. Ward ran into the nursery to check on Chad. She picked him up, held him tightly, and murmured, "Oh, my baby, my baby. Are you all right?"

Awakened by his mother's words, Chad responded by starting to cry. Once she realized the baby was okay, Mrs. Ward calmed down and thanked Kay for her life-saving actions.

"Oh, I almost forgot," Kay told her. "Here's the locket. But I have no idea how it got into his mouth."

"I think I know," said Mrs. Ward. "The locket was on a chain I wore around my neck. The clasp wasn't very good. When I put Chad down for the night, the chain must have broken and I hadn't realized it. The locket probably fell into the crib. When Chad woke up later, he put it in his mouth."

Kay wanted to tell her about the old woman, but she didn't dare. She thought the Wards would think she was crazy. As Mr. Ward was about to drive her home, Kay's curiosity got the best of her.

"Mrs. Ward, when I pulled the locket out of Chad's throat, I couldn't help but open it up. I noticed there was a photo of an old woman. Who is she?"

"That's my mother."

"Does she live around here?"

"No, dear." Mrs. Ward's eyes started to get misty. "She died of cancer just before Chad was born."

The color seemed to drain from Kay's face. *I was awakened by the ghost of Chad's grandmother! And she helped me save her grandson's life!*

"It was such a shame, because she was really looking forward to being a grandmother for the first time," said Mrs. Ward. "She would have been so good to him. She was such a caring person. I miss her. I wish she were here."

"Believe me, Mrs. Ward," said Kay, "she's here in spirit!"

THE SCAREDY CATS

They didn't mean to do it.

Oh sure, the three boys admitted they were chasing the cat for fun. But they didn't mean for the tabby to run out in the street and get killed by a car.

Now they were about to pay for the untimely death of that poor animal in a most unusual way.

———

High school freshmen Nick Grissom, Bill Hardy, and Dave Lund weren't the kind of boys who caused trouble. Then again, they weren't exactly angels. They each had been slapped with a detention during the year for minor offenses in class — Bill for deliberately belching, Dave for falling asleep, and Nick for reading a comic book. But that was it.

One afternoon, the boys were walking down an alley in their neighborhood when they spotted a large gray tabby with dirty, matted hair. Her muddy hind legs were on the edge of an open garbage can as she stuck her head and paws inside and began chewing on a chicken bone.

"I hate that cat," said Bill. "She's always yowling outside my window."

"Who does it belong to?" asked Nick.

"It's just a stray," answered Bill.

"Let's sneak up and scare her," Dave suggested.

The boys quietly crept closer and closer while the cat continued to gnaw the chicken off the bone. But when they closed in, her ears perked up. She glanced behind her and, with a hiss, leaped to the ground and scampered down the alley with the boys in hot pursuit.

She zigged left and zagged right. She climbed up and over Mrs. Gilmore's wood fence and darted through the Lees' vegetable garden. But the boys were still on her tail. She tore under the Starks' backyard picnic table, took a sharp turn at the driveway, and then tried to make a mad dash across the street.

The boys had just ran past the picnic table when they heard the screeching of car tires. They turned at the driveway and came to a sudden halt. There, in the street, lay the cat. Dead.

"Oh, man," moaned Nick. "Look what we did."

"It's no big deal," said Bill coldly. "The cat was a stray. She was probably sick, starving, and had fleas. It's just as well the car put her out of her misery. Now I can get some peace and quiet at night."

"I still feel kind of sad," said Nick.

"It wasn't our fault," Dave said. "The cat should have looked both ways before crossing the street."

The boys laughed and headed down the street to the convenience store for a soda. But they wouldn't be laughing for long.

That night, Bill was in bed and about to fall asleep when the irritating howling of a cat broke the silence. "YEEOOOWWWLL . . . YEEOOOWWWLL."

Not that cat again! thought Bill. *Wait, it can't be. She's dead. Great! Just when you get rid of one cat, another one comes along.* He opened his window and looked in his

61

backyard. Only then did he realize the yowling wasn't coming from outside. It sounded like the cat was right in his room! But he and his mother didn't own a pet. Bill looked under the bed, behind the dresser, and in his closet. He found no cat.

Bill walked into the other bedroom where his mom was sound asleep. Then he checked the kitchen and living room. He was really getting annoyed because the yowling — a strange mixture of a high-pitched wail and a loud howl — followed him wherever he went. He grabbed a flashlight and peeked in the attic. But he saw and heard nothing there.

Somewhere inside the house, the constant "YEEOOOWWWLL . . . YEEOOOWWWLL" grated on Bill until he could hardly stand it. He finally dove into his bed and covered his ears with his pillow until the yowling finally faded away a few hours later.

Meanwhile, a block away, Dave was jarred awake by a menacing hissing sound that grew louder and louder. He searched high and low throughout the house but couldn't find the source of the noise. Every time he thought he was getting closer, the hissing stopped.

Two houses away, Nick tossed and turned in his sleep. Whenever he started to dream, he was repeatedly inter-rupted by mewing — the kind of sound a frightened, lost kitten would make.

When they met at school the next morning, the boys didn't say anything about their sleepless nights. They were too involved in making plans for the weekend and trying to find out more about the new girl in class.

Later that day, Bill was setting the dinner table when he heard a meow. "I don't know where that cat is," he told his mother, "but when I find it, I'll —"

"Eeeek!" she screamed. "Get it out of here!" She hopped onto the kitchen chair and kept shrieking. Bill had never seen his mother so scared or move so fast.

"What is it, Mom?" He followed her gaze to the floor where a black snake was slithering across the kitchen. He shuddered at the sight because he hated snakes.

"Get rid of it!" she cried. "Do something!"

Bill grabbed a broom and shooed the nonpoisonous reptile outside. As he watched it crawl away, he noticed it had teeth marks halfway between its head and tail, as if an animal had bitten it.

"Where did that come from?" she asked.

"I don't know. It had to come in through an open door or basement window."

"Well, I did have the door propped open for a bit while I was cleaning," she said.

Neither felt like eating dinner that night.

About the same time, Dave was home stretched out on the floor resting on a pillow and watching TV with his younger brother. "Hey, quit tickling me," Dave snapped at his brother.

"I'm not touching you."

"Then who's playing with my hair?" Dave sat up, turned around, and yelled, *"Aaahhh!"* A rat, bleeding from its sides, was scurrying around the room.

Meanwhile, Nick was home washing up for dinner. As he looked at himself in the bathroom mirror, he reached for a bar of soap. But what he felt wasn't soap. His hand jerked away and he let out a yelp. It was a dead bird — one with teeth marks on its back.

"You won't believe what happened at our house," Bill told his buddies the next day. "There was a snake in our kitchen. We were just getting ready to eat when my mother

63

started screaming and freaking out. She jumped up on the chair and wouldn't come down until I swept the snake out the door."

"Yeah, well guess what happened to me," said Dave. "I'm laying on the floor watching TV, and a rat starts picking at my hair! How's that for disgusting?"

"Something funny's going on, here," said Nick. "I found a dead bird on my bathroom sink."

"You know what?" said Bill. "I think somebody's playing tricks on us."

"Maybe you're right," Dave said. "Who have we ticked off lately? Who's sneaky enough to slip those animals in our houses?"

"What about Jeff Taft?" said Nick. "Bill, you really put him down the other day in front of all the cheerleaders."

"Well, he had it coming," Bill said. "But Jeff wouldn't have gotten back at all three of us. Come on, think. Who would have done this to us?"

"I don't know, but if I catch him, look out," said Dave. "Revenge will be s-o-o-o-o sweet."

That evening, Bill was helping his mother put dinner on the table. As he carried a bowl of spaghetti, he felt something soft and furry brush up against his leg and snag his pants cuff. Bill tripped and belly-flopped on the floor as the bowl flew through the air and smashed against the wall. As spaghetti sauce and noodles began sliding down the wall, his mother shouted, "William Thomas Hardy, how clumsy can you get! You've ruined our dinner!"

"I'm sorry, Mom, but something tripped me. I could swear it was a cat."

"A cat? There's no cat around here. Do you see a cat?"

"Well, no, but . . :"

"Help me clean up this mess."

64

Meanwhile, Dave was taking out the garbage. As he walked past a hedge toward the alley, he cried out in pain. Four deep cuts, parallel and close to each other, began to bleed on his forearm. It looked as if something had raked across his skin, slicing it open.

About an hour later, Nick was dozing on the couch when he awoke to a frightening sensation. He felt something furry covering his mouth and nose, and he couldn't breathe. Frantically, he tried to get the thing off his face, but there was nothing there. In desperation, he rolled off the couch and finally was able to breathe again.

The next morning at school, before the first bell rang, Nick told his two buddies, "A lot of weird stuff has been happening, at least to me, and I've been doing some thinking. The other night, after the cat was killed, I kept hearing strange mewing sounds in my dreams."

"I couldn't even get to sleep that night," said Bill. "There was a cat howling up a storm, and it sounded like it was inside my house. It sounded like it was inside the walls."

"I kept hearing a cat hissing," added Dave.

"Okay," said Nick, getting more excited. "I think we're on to something. The next day, what happens? Bill, a snake gets into your kitchen. Dave's got a rat playing in his hair. And I find a dead bird. Now, what do they all have in common?" The boys gave him a blank stare.

"Those are the kind of animals a cat brings into the house," he said.

"Now that you mention it," said Dave, "the rat was bleeding."

"The snake had bite marks on it," said Bill.

"And so did the bird!" declared Nick.

"Oh, man, this is getting too freaky," Dave said.

"Follow me on this," said Nick. "Did anything strange happen to you last night, Bill?"

"Yeah, my mom blew a gasket because I was carrying the bowl of spaghetti to the dinner table and tripped, and the spaghetti went flying." His eyes grew wide. "You know, it felt like a cat had tripped me. Except there was no cat."

"Dave, what about you?" Nick asked.

"Nothing much. I was taking the garbage out and cut my arm on something, but I don't know what did it. Here, look."

"Those look like claw marks to me," said Nick. "Something strange happened to me too. I was taking a nap after dinner when it felt like an invisible cat was trying to smother me. Dave, remember the other day when you said revenge was sweet?"

"Yeah, so?"

"What if that cat came back for revenge?" asked Nick.

"That's impossible," said Bill. "We saw her get killed. She's dead."

"Guys, I know you're going to think I'm crazy, but what if. . ." Nick hesitated because he didn't want his pals to laugh at him. "What if the things that have happened to us were caused by the ghost of that cat? What if she's haunting us?"

"Are you crazy?" said Dave.

"Man, you've got cat hair in your brain," Bill declared.

"Do you have a better explanation?"

"Not really, but we know someone who might," said Bill. "Let's ask Mr. Pratt. He's pretty cool." The boys marched off to see Ray Pratt, one of their school's most popular teachers. He always had a ready ear and a quick response for any student who had a problem.

After they told Mr. Pratt everything that had happened, he stroked his chin and said, "Let's look at this thing logically. It's certainly possible that a snake, a rat, and a bird could get into a house through an open window or door. It's also possible those animals were brought in by a cat. The noises you heard could have been from a real cat. They can get into crawl spaces under houses so when they howl or meow they sound like they're inside the walls. Now, about those other incidents. Bill, you could have simply tripped over your own feet. Nick, you could have been dreaming you were suffocating. And Dave, that cut on your arm could have been caused by walking past a thorny bush."

"Are you saying it wasn't a ghost?" asked Nick. "These are all just coincidences?"

"Sometimes when the mind is troubled, it ties unrelated events together and forms a conclusion that logically may not make a lot of sense," said Mr. Pratt.

"Troubled mind?" said Nick. "You mean like a guilty conscience?"

"You said it, I didn't," replied Mr. Pratt.

The teacher's explanation made sense to the boys, and they vowed to forget about the ghostly cat. Then they really teased Nick for even suggesting that a cat could haunt them. And to think they almost believed him!

After school, they went over to Bill's house to raid the refrigerator. As they sat down at the kitchen table, Dave asked, "Bill, you don't have a cat, do you?"

"You know I don't."

"Then what are these cat prints doing all over the table?"

Sure enough, the table top was covered with muddy cat tracks. But that's not what left the boys so thunderstruck. They discovered that the paw prints came from

67

nowhere and led to nowhere. There were none on the floor around the table and none anywhere else in the room!

When Nick, Dave, and Bill finally recovered from their shock, they made a solemn promise to each other never again to treat any animal badly.

From that day on, none of the boys experienced anything strange involving a mysterious, unseen cat.

THE THING
IN THE ATTIC

Maria Blanco and her sister Sonia were thrilled when their family moved into the big, century-old Victorian house. For their hard-working parents, Jorge and Theresa, it was a dream come true. The home had two fireplaces, a hand-carved bannister, and even a secret wall panel for hiding valuable stuff.

It had a third-story attic that Maria, 13, and Sonia, 12, turned into their special room. The sisters taped posters to the slanted walls. They displayed their teddy bear and miniature horse collections in the attic's many nooks and crannies. Best of all, the girls were able to play their stereo full blast up there without bothering their parents.

It seemed like the perfect teenagers' room . . . but it wasn't really. It held a frightening secret that to this day has never been solved.

One rainy afternoon, while listening to the top-40 countdown on the radio, the girls were sitting on the attic floor tossing a tennis ball back and forth. They kept flinging it harder and harder with each throw to see who would drop it first. Eventually, Maria fired a fastball that bounced off Sonia's hands and slammed into the wall. But the ball didn't bounce back. It went through the wall!

69

The sisters looked at each other in astonishment. "Wow, what an arm!" said Sonia, laughing.

When they went to investigate, they discovered that part of the wall was not made of plaster. It was canvas painted white that had become brittle with age. Maria carefully peeled back the canvas. "Look at this, Sonia!"

About two feet (.6 m) behind the canvas was a small wooden door no taller than a yardstick and a little over a foot (.3 m) wide. It had an iron latch and a handle secured by an old rusty padlock.

"I wonder what's in there," said Maria. "And I wonder why this fake wall is in front of it."

"Let's tell Mom and Dad," said Sonia. "When Dad comes home from work, we'll get him to saw off the lock."

"I don't know if telling them is a good idea. This could be the entrance to some kind of secret room or passageway. We already know about their hiding place in the hallway. This could be our own secret hiding place. Let's not tell anyone about it just yet."

"Okay," Sonia said warily. "It's kind of spooky-looking, though."

"Yeah, but it's kind of exciting too."

They tromped down to the basement and brought back their father's toolbox and a hacksaw. For 15 tiring minutes the girls took turns sawing the padlock until finally it broke.

"All right! It's off!" shouted Maria triumphantly. Grabbing hold of the latch, she asked, "Are you ready to see what's inside?"

"What if it's a dead body?" asked Sonia. "Or like that dead mother in the rocking chair in the movie *Psycho*?"

"What if it's hidden treasure?"

Maria lifted the latch and yanked on the handle. But nothing happened. "Help me, Sonia. I can't move it."

Despite the efforts of the two girls, the door wouldn't budge. "Well, no wonder," said Maria. "It's nailed shut. You can barely see the heads of the nails."

The girls spent the next two hours chipping away at the wood and then prying out a dozen big nails. Sweaty and tired, the sisters were finally ready to open the door.

"I don't know what's in there, but someone must have thought it was pretty important," said Maria.

"Are you sure we should be opening this without calling Mom or Dad?" asked Sonia. "I mean, what if it's something really awful in there? What if there's a monster?"

"Come on, Sonia, don't be a chicken." With her heart pounding with excitement — and a touch of fear — Maria lifted the latch and pulled on the handle. "Well, here goes." Reluctantly, the door slowly creaked open.

As Sonia got ready to cover her eyes in case there was something terrible inside, Maria took a quick peek. Then she crawled inside.

"What do you see? What do you see?" asked Sonia anxiously.

"Well, it could be something really neat and then again maybe nothing," came the reply. "Come on in."

The mystery door led to a musty, tiny room with a ceiling too low for the girls to stand up. But it did have a small window that apparently no one had noticed from the ground before.

The room was empty except for one thing — an old wooden trunk with a curved lid. It was wrapped in a chain attached to a rusty padlock. "This could be our treasure," said Maria.

"Or body parts," added Sonia.

"Oh, stop with the dead bodies, will you? Go get me the saw and let's cut this chain."

This time the girls made short work of the chain. Now it was time to open up the trunk. Standing as far away as she could while still holding the lid, Maria slowly and carefully opened it. Then she inched closer and peered inside.

"Well, will you look at this?" Maria said. She pulled out a gold container about the size and shape of a water pitcher. It had no spout or handle

"What is it?" asked Sonia.

"I think it's an urn," Maria replied. She lifted the lid off the container and noticed it was filled with ashes. "It's a burial urn all right."

"See, it was a dead body. I was right," gloated Sonia.

"What a bummer," said Maria. "I wonder who it was. There's no inscription or anything." After inspecting the urn, she put it back into the trunk and shut the lid.

After they closed the door to the room, the sisters agreed to wait a few days before telling their parents. Maria wanted the extra time to think of a way they could use the secret room to pull a practical joke on them.

But there would be nothing funny in the Blanco household over the next two nights. Only terror.

Because Sonia's bedroom was being painted, the sisters slept that night in the twin beds in Maria's room. Sometime around 3 A.M., Maria woke up in confusion and fear, feeling a tremendous weight on her chest. She could hardly breathe. It felt as though some invisible being was on top of her. Maria tried to pound on him, but her hands seemed to go right through the attacker. She tried to scream, but she felt an ice-cold hand cover her mouth.

Panic surged through her body. *He's trying to kill me!* With every ounce of strength left in her body, Maria thrashed on her bed until she tumbled to the floor.

The commotion woke up Sonia. But before she could say or do anything, the evil force gripped her by the throat and began to squeeze until she thought she would choke to death. Just then, Maria crawled to the wall and flicked on the light. The attack was over . . . and there was no one there! The bedroom door was still closed and so were the windows.

The two girls threw themselves into each other's arms and sobbed hysterically until Jorge and Theresa ran into the room. Each parent grabbed a child and comforted her until she had calmed down.

Between sobs and gasps for breath, the girls related their horrible ordeal. At first, it was too hard for their parents to comprehend.

"Is there any way this could have been some terrible nightmare?" asked Jorge.

"How could we both have had the same dream?" said a still-shaking Maria. "And how do you explain this?" She rolled up the sleeve to her nightshirt, revealing huge welts on her forearms. "And this?" she added, pointing to several ugly bruises on her legs.

"Jorge!" exclaimed Theresa. "Look at Sonia's neck!" The skin above her collarbone was red and had the imprint of a pair of giant hands.

The Blancos called the police, who sped to the house and listened to the girls' stories. They examined the room, dusted for fingerprints, and looked around the outside of the house. But there was no evidence of forced entry.

After the police left, Maria and Sonia told their parents about the secret room. Their father immediately bounded

73

up the stairs, crawled into the tiny room, opened the trunk, and examined the urn. Somehow, he felt better knowing the ashes were still inside.

The next night, Jorge sat in a chair in the girls' room, promising to protect them if there was any trouble. After tossing and turning in bed for several hours, the exhausted sisters finally fell asleep. Shortly before 3 A.M., Jorge nodded off too.

That's when the invisible force entered the room again. Maria was roused out of her sleep by an icy hand that clamped onto her foot and jerked her off the bed. She let out a cry of absolute terror. Maria rolled onto the floor, desperately trying to fend off someone or something that no one could see.

Meanwhile, the invisible force had grabbed Sonia by the arm and slammed her against the wall.

By now, Jorge had bolted out of his chair and flipped on the light. Crazed with anger, he began flailing away at the air and snarled, "Fight me, you monster! Take me on! Show yourself, you coward!"

But the unseen evil had quit its attack, leaving both girls curled up in trembling balls of fear in separate corners of the room. Gently, Jorge and Theresa, who had just rushed in, led the girls downstairs to the living room and tried to calm them.

The next day, while the family moved in with relatives, Jorge tried to unravel the frightening mystery. He was convinced the evil force was somehow connected to the urn. He hoped to find the identity of the person whose ashes were inside, so he talked to neighbors about the previous owners. But he failed to find any answers.

The girls wanted the urn and the trunk removed before they were willing to return home. But Jorge wasn't

74

convinced that was the right thing to do.

"Maybe whoever is in that urn felt violated when you girls discovered the room," he told them. "Maybe this ghost just wants to be left alone. If we move the urn, where will we take it? And what other terrible things will happen to us if we do? Let me try something else first."

Jorge went to the hardware store for some supplies. When he returned, he walked up to the third-floor attic and into the tiny room. He made sure the urn was closed. Then he shut the trunk, carefully wrapped a new chain around it, and secured it with a new padlock.

After he crawled out and closed the door, Jorge clamped on a new lock and nailed boards across it. To seal it for good, he bricked up the fake canvas wall.

"I know it's crazy," he told his family, "but I have no other solutions."

While Maria, Sonia, and their mother remained with relatives, Jorge and his three brothers — all former football players in high school — slept in the house for the next week without incident.

The evil force never returned.

Jorge's most difficult task was trying to convince his family to return to the house he so loved. "Nothing is going to harm you — or this house — while I'm around," he promised.

Reluctantly the family returned, but Maria and Sonia could not bring themselves to ever play in the third-floor attic again. For nearly a year afterwards, they slept in Sonia's bedroom. But eventually they learned to love the house again. Whenever they felt edgy, their father assured them that the house would always remain safe.

However, seven years later, tragedy struck the Blancos — Jorge died of a heart attack.

Since both girls were in college at the time, Theresa decided to move. She bought a smaller home in the same neighborhood and sold the Victorian house to the Farrells, a young family with three small children. Theresa chose not to tell them about the secret room or their haunting ordeal. She didn't want to worry them. Besides, she was convinced the evil force was sealed up in the attic for good.

About a year later, Theresa bumped into Mrs. Farrell at the grocery store and asked if everything was all right with her family and the house.

"You didn't tell us the whole truth about the house," said Mrs. Farrell.

"What are you talking about?" asked Theresa.

"Come on, Mrs. Blanco. Surely you must have seen the ghost?"

"You saw the ghost?" she said with a gasp.

"We've spotted him a couple of times by the stairs leading up to the third-floor attic."

"Has he harmed or scared anyone?"

"Oh, we were startled at first. But he seems nice. All he does is smile and then he fades away."

"What does he look like?"

"About six feet tall, broad shoulders, dark wavy hair combed back, a thick mustache —"

"Yes, Mrs. Farrell, I know the ghost well," said Theresa with tears welling up in her eyes. "He always said he'd make sure no harm came to that house. You see, you just described my dead husband!"

THE WARNING

Dylan Lang and his cousin Greg Arnold would be dead if it hadn't been for the warning — a warning so creepy it still sends shivers up their spines.

A few years ago, when they were 16 years old, they spent their spring break with an uncle in his cabin in northern California. They loved hiking among the tall pines, spotting deer and foxes. But most of all they loved to fish in the streams.

On the last day of their vacation, before heading home to Los Angeles, Dylan and Greg walked a mile from their uncle's cabin toward Cooper Creek. The stream snaked through a narrow ravine, tumbled over huge rocks, spilled over small waterfalls, and swirled in waist-deep pools.

Dressed in flannel shirts and sleeveless jackets, the boys followed a winding path in a forest shrouded in a thick, chilly fog. After they passed the only other home in the remote area — a log cabin built into the side of a monstrous boulder — they reached the ravine.

Clutching their fishing gear, Dylan and Greg scrambled down the steep, 30-foot (9-m) embankment to a sandbar that jutted out of the water. It offered a perfect place for them to sit and watch their poles. They could see several sunfish and small bass swimming in the crystal-clear water. But the primary target for the boys were chubs — fish about 4-12 inches (10-30 cm) long.

While baiting their hooks with pieces of hot dogs, Dylan, the more experienced fisherman of the two, told Greg, "Chubs are quick to bite, but they're difficult to hook. You have to pay attention to see them bite — and then you need quick hands to set the hook."

"A dollar says I catch more than you," Greg challenged.

"A dollar?" Dylan responded mockingly. "Let's make it worthwhile. Five bucks. And a dollar for the first catch of the day."

"You're on!"

Not more than 15 minutes after they arrived came the first sign that this day would be one they'd never forget. A strange voice, so faint that only Dylan detected it above the gurgling water, whispered, "Get out of here!"

Dylan turned to Greg and asked, "What did you say?"

"I didn't say anything," replied Greg as he dropped his line in the water.

A minute later the voice — this time a little louder but still hoarse — repeated, "Get out of here!"

"There, did you hear that?" Dylan asked his cousin.

"Yeah, I heard something. It sounded like a little boy whispering, but I couldn't make out what he said."

Greg and Dylan stuck their poles in the sandbar and scanned the ravine. They saw nothing among the shrubs and trees nor along the barren banks of rocks and sand. The cousins stood silent for a moment, but the only sounds they heard where the rippling of the water and the rustling of the trees.

They went back to fishing, and before long Greg reeled in a six-inch (15-cm) chub. "The first catch of the day!" he boasted as he released the little fish. "You owe me a buck."

"You're not going to count that little thing, are you?" said Dylan. "Where's your pride? It's got to be at least ten inches (25 cm) to count."

"Hey, are you trying to welch on our bet? Now pay up or I'll — Look! Across the bank." At the edge of the creek stood a skinny boy about ten years old with a short haircut. He had on a plain yellow T-shirt, blue jeans with red patches on both knees, and black high tops. And he was soaking wet. He slowly raised his hand, pointed to the boys and, with no expression on his face or emotion in his hoarse voice, warned, "Get out of here!"

This time, both boys clearly heard him. "Why? What's the matter?" asked Greg.

"There's danger," the boy responded. Then he took one step back and disappeared into the shrubs.

"Hey, wait!" shouted Dylan. "What danger? Where? Who are you?"

There was no reply. Turning to Greg, he asked, "What do you make of that?"

"It's just some kid trying to scare us. He probably doesn't like us here and wants the creek all to himself. This is our last day up here, so let's get back to fishing."

About ten minutes later, they noticed the same boy, still dripping wet, standing a few feet away from them on the sandbar.

"You again," said Greg. "Why do you want us to get out of here?"

"There's danger," the boy answered. "There's going to be a flash flood."

"When?" asked Dylan.

"Soon."

"How do you know?"

"I know."

79

The boys found the kid weird — real weird, almost zombie-like. His lips hardly moved when he talked, and he spoke in a whispered monotone. He had a glazed, far-away stare, and he never made eye contact. Also, his face seemed drained of all color.

"Just who are you anyway?" asked Greg.

"I'm Bobby Randall."

"Why are you all wet?"

"I fell in."

"You ought to get those wet clothes off," said Greg. "You must be freezing. Do you live far from here?"

"I came from the cabin with the big boulder."

Suddenly, they heard a whining sound. The reel on one of the poles that had been resting on a Y-shaped branch in the sand was spinning crazily.

"Hey, Greg!" yelled Dylan. "There goes your fishing pole!" A bass had hit the bait and was about to swim off with the pole. Greg ran into the frigid water, retrieved his pole, and then reeled in a two-pound (.9 kg) bass.

"How's that for luck?" he gloated. "There's my fish story for the day." Looking around, he said, "Hey, where's that kid Bobby?"

"Beats me," said Dylan, shaking his head.

"Man, that's one bizarre dude."

"You've got that right," agreed Dylan. He glanced down at the footprints in the sand and then nudged Greg. "This is really strange. How many sets of footprints do you see in the sand leading from the bank to here?"

"Two — yours and mine."

"Right. So where are Bobby's? He couldn't have walked up to us from out of the water because we were facing the stream and would have seen him. The kid has to weigh at least 70 pounds (32 kg), which means he should have left some footprints in the sand. So how come we don't see any?"

"You're freaking me out," said Greg. "What do you say we get out of here. It's cold and starting to drizzle anyway."

As they gathered up their gear, they heard Bobby's eerie voice for the last time. "There's danger. Get out of here." They had no idea where the voice was coming from. With their poles and their fish in hand, they scrambled quickly up the steep ravine. As they neared the top, they heard a rumbling sound coming from further up the creek. The noise grew louder and louder until it turned into a thunderous rampage.

A deadly wall of churning water six feet (1.8 m) high roared around the bend in the creek and swept over the sandbar — right where the boys had just been fishing! Bushes, shrubs, and small trees were torn from their roots as the raging water wiped out everything in its path.

"It's a flash flood!" shouted Dylan. "If we had stayed just a couple of minutes longer, we'd have drowned for sure!"

Before the boys had a chance to mull over their narrow escape from death, they saw a sickening sight. The seething torrent had snared Bobby and was whisking him downstream. With his arms flailing about, Bobby slammed into a boulder and disappeared under the water, surfaced briefly, and then was carried out of sight.

"We've got to help him!" shouted Greg.

"We can't outrun the current," said Dylan. "Let's get to that cabin over there." They raced to the house built into the boulder and pounded on the door.

A bearded, balding man in his forties with a frayed lumberjack shirt, jeans, and boots answered. "Please, mister," pleaded Dylan. "Call the police or the fire department or someone. A boy is drowning! He got caught in a flash flood!"

The man reeled for a moment as if the words had nearly knocked him out. A pained look creased his face.

"Please, mister, please call!" cried Greg.

The man snapped out of his trance, grabbed the phone, and called the sheriff's office. "Sam? This is Harry. Some boys here tell me they saw a boy get swept away by a flash flood in Cooper Creek."

Harry paused and shook his head when the sheriff told him he had just received a call from a fisherman reporting that a retaining dam had burst for the second time in two years. Harry choked up with emotion and slumped into his chair. "I know, Sam. It's like reliving that nightmare." He hung up the phone as tears streamed down his face.

"He said his name was Bobby," Greg told Harry. "And I think he said he lived here."

Harry bounded out of his chair. "What did you say?"

"The boy. He said his name was Bobby."

"Bobby what?"

"I don't remember," Greg said.

"Was his name Randall? Bobby Randall?"

"Yeah, that's it."

"What did he look like?"

"He was kind of a skinny kid about ten years old. A short haircut, a yellow T-shirt —"

"And jeans with bright red patches on the knee?"

"Yeah, how did you know?"

"You just described my son!"

"Oh, I'm so sorry to hear that. I sure hope he makes it."

There was no way for Greg and Dylan to prepare for what happened next. Harry's eyes flashed with anger. He grabbed his hunting rifle and leveled it right at the two stunned boys.

"All right, you punks!" he snarled. "That is the meanest, dirtiest joke I've ever heard. Have you no shame? No decency? I ought to kill you right now!"

"What are you talking about, mister?" Dylan shouted in panic. "Your son's fighting for his life in a flash flood out there, and you want to kill us? Are you nuts?"

"My son's not fighting for his life," Harry snapped back. "He's dead!"

"How do you know?" said Greg. "Don't ever give up hope. Maybe he caught a branch or got washed up on the bank or —"

"He died two years ago," Harry said. "A flash flood in Cooper Creek swept him away. They found his body four miles downstream by Bloodworth Bridge."

The boys shook their heads in disbelief. "That's impossible," said Dylan. "We saw him while we were fishing. He came by to warn us at least three times. If it hadn't been for him, we would have been caught in the flash flood and drowned."

Harry lowered his gun and sobbed uncontrollably. When he finally regained his composure, he murmured, "My son, my son . . . Is it possible he came back from the dead — to save your lives?"

THE GLOWING
BALL OF DEATH

The Spicer twins, Maggie and Molly, had heard the scary stories about the mysterious white ball of light for at least three years. What made the accounts so eerie was that the girls heard them from adults, not kids.

Their mail carrier reported seeing it. So did their former first grade teacher, and their father's good friend, the bank president. They all claimed to have spotted a large ball of light about three feet (.9 m) wide hovering over the Dempsey house at night. The bizarre light would then slowly drift into the forest where the stunned witnesses lost sight of it.

The first time anyone had seen the strange ball of light was right after the murder.

———

Mr. and Mrs. Dempsey were Vermont farmers who, for as long as anyone could remember, had lived in a narrow two-story house at the end of a dirt road. They kept to themselves, so people didn't know much about them other than that the couple raised hay, alfalfa, and corn on their farm. When the Dempseys retired, they stayed put, leasing the land to other farmers. Meanwhile, the couple, who had a reputation for being miserly, let their house fall into disrepair.

The last time Maggie and Molly saw them was when the girls were 12 years old and had gone over to the Dempsey house with their mother to deliver freshly baked cookies. Although Mr. Dempsey didn't say much, he did smile and compliment the girls on how pretty they looked.

The murder occurred a few months later. The mail carrier, Cindy Smith, was the first to notice something was wrong when the Dempseys' mailbox filled up. Because she knew the couple never went away for more than a day or two, Cindy decided to investigate. The doors were locked, so she peeked through the windows. When she looked into the living room, she cried out in horror — Mrs. Dempsey's body lay on the floor. The police found she had been shot to death with a handgun. There was no sign of her husband. However, a suitcase and some of his clothes were missing. And so was their old station wagon.

The murder shocked the residents of the nearby town and surrounding area. Especially upset was the Spicer family, who lived on an apple orchard just half a mile (.8 km) away from the Dempseys in this otherwise peaceful valley.

For a year after the killing, David and Beth Spicer wouldn't let their twins go off by themselves. But as time passed without any major crime in the area (other than the theft of some farm machinery), the Spicers gave the twins more freedom to explore on their own. Fears of a killer on the loose had subsided. Most everyone assumed Mr. Dempsey had murdered his wife and then taken off for parts unknown.

On a gloomy Saturday afternoon three years after the murder, Maggie and Molly, who were now 15, wanted to do something new, different, and exciting. They were always game for anything — jumping fences on horseback, canoeing down rapids, skiing backwards.

"I've got it!" Maggie told her sister. "Let's go snoop around the Dempsey house."

"Great idea," said Molly. "Maybe we'll find a clue to the murder."

"Or that mysterious light."

With their beagle Sparky tagging along, the girls — bundled up in ski jackets to ward off the fall chill — jogged over to the scene of the crime. The house, which had been boarded up since the murder, tilted slightly to one side where the foundation had cracked and the roof sagged over the porch. What little paint remained on the house had peeled, allowing the weathered wooden siding and windowsills to rot.

It didn't take much effort to pry open the long-unused front door and slip inside. The dusty rooms, which had been emptied of furniture, were netted with spider webs. The rickety wood floor creaked with every step. Everything in the house appeared in shades of somber gray because the late afternoon light had trouble penetrating the dirty, streaked windows.

"It's kind of spooky in here, isn't it?" said Molly.

"It gives me the chills," Maggie answered. Bending down, she pointed to a large dark stain on the living-room floor and said, "Oh, gross. This is probably where Mrs. Dempsey was shot and bled to death."

Suddenly the door to the kitchen slammed shut with a loud bang. Both girls screamed in surprise. "Oh, that scared me," said Maggie with a nervous laugh. "I didn't feel a breeze in here, did you?"

"No," said Molly. "Let's go check it out." But when she tried to open the kitchen door, the knob wouldn't turn. "That's funny. It's locked."

She looked down to see Sparky stick his nose under

86

the door and sniff. Molly thought she saw a streak of light coming from under the other side of the door just when Sparky began to whine and back away. Then, with his tail tucked between his legs and the hair on his back standing on end, the dog gave a halfhearted growl and scampered out the open front door.

"Ohhh-kaaaay," said Molly, carefully backpedaling from the kitchen door. "I think that's our cue to split." The twins scurried out of the house and bounded into the freshly cut hay field that separated the Dempseys' land from the Spicers' orchard.

"That place gave me the creeps," said Maggie.

"Me too," said Molly with a shudder. They began walking around the large bales of hay that dotted the field when Molly looked around for their dog. "Hey, where's Sparky? He was here just a minute ago."

Behind one of the bales, Sparky began howling in a way they had never heard before. It sounded so fearful. "There's something wrong with Sparky!" Maggie cried.

When the girls rushed back, they found their beagle cowering in the dirt. "What's the matter, boy?" asked Molly. The dog was shaking and howling, his terror-crazed eyes locked on the roof of the house a few hundred yards away. As Molly gently stroked the dog's back, Maggie grabbed her sister's arm and in a trembling voice said, "Molly, do you see what I see?"

In the dusk, against a sky darkened by the clouds, a bright ball of light hovered just above the chimney. At first, it looked like a large helium balloon. But the awestruck girls knew it couldn't be, because it emitted its own light and changed shape from perfectly round to oblong to the squashed look of a floating pumpkin.

"That's the ball of light people have been talking

about!" said Maggie. "What do you suppose it is?"

Before Molly could speak, the ball of light began to move. It drifted away from the house and disappeared among the trees that bordered the hay field.

"Do you believe this? We actually saw it!" said Maggie, feeling thrilled and scared at the same time.

"I can't wait to tell Mom and Dad!" added Molly.

When they burst into their kitchen minutes later, the twins jabbered excitedly to their parents about the mysterious light. At first the Spicers thought their daughters were putting them on. But the look of amazement in the girls' eyes convinced David and Beth their children were telling the truth.

"I don't know what to make of it, kids," said Beth. "I know others have seen the same thing, but I'd rather we kept a low profile on this, okay?"

The girls reluctantly agreed — sort of. They did tell their friend Kate, but only after she promised to keep it a secret. Not surprisingly, it took only about two days before the whole town heard about it! Some laughed, some scoffed. But most didn't know what to believe.

A week later, after dinner one moonless night, the girls were looking at the planet Saturn through their telescope when off in the distance they spotted the weird ball of light dancing low in the sky.

"Let's follow it!" said Maggie.

"I wish Mom and Dad were home," said Molly. "But why not? Let's take Sparky and go."

They ran through the orchard and reached the hay field, where the light was floating toward the woods. With Sparky whining and growling at the twins' feet, the girls followed the glowing ball from a cautious distance. It effortlessly weaved its way through the trees and then eased down until it was just above the base of a maple tree. The light seemed to defy physics because, unlike a torch or beam, it did not illuminate anything around it.

The girls bravely inched forward and were about 20 yards (18 m) away when Sparky came to a halt and started howling in the same fearful way he had the week before.

As Maggie turned around and tried to comfort the beagle, Molly let out an ear-piercing shriek, turned on her heels, and started to run. Maggie and Sparky were right behind her. When they reached the clearing, they stopped.

"Why did you scream?" asked Maggie.

"I thought I saw the face of a man — an ugly, horrible face, and his mouth was all twisted."

"I didn't see any face. Your imagination must have gotten the best of you." Poking Molly playfully in the ribs with her elbow, Maggie added, "Scaredy cat."

"Well, if I'm such a scaredy cat, how come you ran too?" asked Molly.

"Because the only thing that scared me was your screaming. Let's go back."

The girls crept back and, hiding behind a tree, watched uneasily as the ball of light swayed by the base of the maple tree.

"Look!" said Molly. "It's doing it again!" The ball seemed to glimmer, and then a face within it slowly came into view. It was the wrinkled face of an old man. His eyes were shut tight, while his mouth spread wide in a silent scream of torment.

"That face looks like Mr. Dempsey!" said Maggie.

"Is that his ghost?" asked Molly.

"How could it be? He's not dead — or at least he's not supposed to be."

"Whether he is or isn't, I'll bet there's some connection between the light and Mrs. Dempsey's murder."

"Do you think the light is trying to tell us something?"

Before Molly could answer, the face, light, and ball simply vanished.

Later, when their parents came home, the girls recounted what had happened. The following night, at the twins' urging, David and Beth stood with their daughters on their porch roof and, with binoculars, scanned the area for the ball of light. They didn't have long to wait. They spotted it poised above the Dempseys' house.

The family hurried down to the hay field and then followed the glowing ball as it headed for the same spot in the woods, stopping at the base of the same maple tree. The face appeared in the ball and then it all disappeared.

Later that night, as the family sat around the kitchen table sipping on apple cider, they discussed their next step. Despite Beth's concerns that the townspeople would think the family was crazy, David decided to talk to the police.

The next morning he went to the sheriff's office and told Detective Mike Ferraro about the mystery light. Although Ferraro found the story too fantastic to believe, he joined the Spicers that night and saw the glowing ball himself.

"I don't want you to say anything about this to anyone," the detective told the Spicers, "especially you girls, okay? If word gets out that the police are investigating the ball of light, this place will be crawling with sightseers and ghost hunters and who knows what else. It will turn into a circus. I don't know what's going on, but I'm going to get to the bottom of this. There's a reason why the light is going to that particular tree."

The next morning, Ferraro returned to the woods with several deputies and started to dig by the maple tree. When the girls arrived on the scene, Ferraro stopped them and whispered, "Look, I didn't tell these guys about the light. They'd think I was nuts. I told them I got a tip on the Dempsey murder case to dig around the tree for a clue, and that I thought it was worth a try. So I'm counting on you not to say anything."

"Detective!" shouted one of the deputies. "I think we found something." They scooped away more dirt and uncovered a worm-eaten suitcase full of decayed clothes. Then the deputies dug deeper until they found something wrapped in plastic. Inside were the skeletal remains of a body!

Later that day, authorities used dental records to confirm what the Spicer girls already suspected — the body was Mr. Dempsey's. Everyone now knew the old man was not a killer. He had been shot just like his wife. Whoever murdered the couple had tried to make it appear as if Mr. Dempsey had killed his wife and fled.

Although the police scoured the area for other evidence, the case has yet to be solved.

And the eerie ball of light has never returned.

HAUNTED KIDS

$2.95 U.S.
$3.95 CAN.

Has anyone ever told you the story of the
ghost who saved a child's life? Have you
heard what happened to a boy who knocked
over a cemetery gravestone?
Here's a spine-chilling collection of <u>true</u> ghost
stories that have happened to <u>real</u> kids. But
beware — these eerie stories may keep you
reading long past bedtime!

Watermill Press

ISBN 0-8167-3444-5

50295

9 780816 734443